"Scars"

*The Faith, Courage, and Endurance of
Jerome Martin, Jr.*

by

Jerome Martin, Jr.

published by

Jerome Martin, Jr.
Dallas, Georgia
July 2013

"SCARS"

The Faith, Courage, and Endurance of Jerome Martin, Jr.

Copyright © July 2013 by Jerome Martin, Jr.
Dallas, Georgia 30157

All rights reserved. No part of this book may be reproduced or transmitted in any form or by any means, electronic or mechanical, including photocopying, recording, or by any information storage and retrieval system without permission in writing from the copyright owner.

Published by Jerome Martin, Jr.
E. Nicole Martin [porpeytrey@gmail.com]

Book Layout & Format Editing, and
First Edition Printing by
New Hope Publishing, LLC
Atlanta, Georgia 30331
404-629-0446

Edited by Porsha A. Martin

Cover Illustration by Salina Copeland
Cover Layout/Design by Justin W. Davie

This book may be purchased at Amazon.com

Printed in the United States of America

Library of Congress Card Catalog Number: 9781467582353

ISBN 978-1-4675-8235-3

Table of Contents

PREFACE: A Guide to Overcoming Adversity v
CHAPTER 1: The Beginning 1
CHAPTER 2: Boot Camp 11
CHAPTER 3: The Big Buy Out 15
CHAPTER 4: Young Boy Doing Man Things 25
CHAPTER 5: Learning Life's Lessons 31
CHAPTER 6: Gone Too Soon 39
CHAPTER 7: Sam & Ola Mae Dupree 45
CHAPTER 8: Going to Camp 58
CHAPTER 9: Daddy's Big Girl 63
CHAPTER 10: Power Move 69
CHAPTER 11: All or Nothing 82
CHAPTER 12: It's Storming 90
CHAPTER 13: The Struggle 92
CHAPTER 14: Taking Things for Granted 95
CHAPTER 15: What's for Me Is Just for Me 101
CHAPTER 16: Just Want to Give Thanks 104
CHAPTER 17: Real Talk for Men 107
CHAPTER 18: Children 110
CHAPTER 19: Give Life A Chance! 112

PREFACE: A Guide to Overcoming Adversity

I am a forty five year old man who started keeping a journal to deal with things that were happening in my life. There is a need to provide people with the inspiration and motivation to get back up when they fall. Growing up, times were hard, but we survived. Those times taught me a lot about life. In my early years, some things happened that would help mold and shape me for many years to come. It took about five years to write this, because at times, the pain and emotion were too much to bear. The emotions from this book are what I draw from, when day to day life seems unbearable. Looking back over my journey gives me the strength to continue fighting for the best life for me.

Some people believe my book is about bashing my mom, but she is just part of my story. This is not for people who have a perfect life; it is for those that are searching for answers each and every day. Many of us haven't had someone to sit us down and explain why life has so many curves. The journey in the book gives me a chance to share my good times and sad times.

Living in a city and working in a profession where I have seen many hopeless and lost people mentally, I welcomed the chance to write a book that would hopefully give someone the strength to get up and make a change in their situation. I would like to thank everyone who previewed Chapter 1 and gave their feedback on how powerful and moving my story is. Don't ever give up!

SCARS

By Jerome Martin Jr.

CHAPTER 1: The Beginning

One day we were burning trash in the backyard in a pit. I went out to empty the trash, and stepped on a melted milk jug, which stuck to the bottom of my foot and gave me third degree burns. I doctored on my own foot by putting it in cold water, and day by day, I picked the plastic and chunks of meat out of it. Believe it or not, I never went to the doctor. In those days, people didn't go to the doctor, unless it was a case of life or death.

I was born Jerome Martin Jr. on February 13, 1968, in Tallahassee, Florida, the third of four boys. My brothers and I are pretty much stair steps, ages 4, 6, 7, and 8. The older two are what they call Irish twins: for a week they are the same age. At a very young age we went to live with our grandmother, because our mom decided to run off with a low life that she would later marry. It was very hard to understand how she could just leave us in the middle of the night and not even say good-bye. That hurt me so bad. Upon reaching adulthood

The Beginning

myself, it is easier to realize how a man can have that much influence on a woman. Years would pass, and no phone calls, not even on Christmas. We would sit, sometimes in the woods, where we often played, talked, and cried, and wonder why she would leave us alone. Did she not love us anymore? This caused me and my brothers to become even closer.

Our mom was a party girl. She hung out in a couple of places called Frenchtown and Hawks. The element in those places wasn't very good. There was an incident where a lady was shooting at my mom's friend. Killing my mom's friend, the bullet went through her head and hit my mom in the arm, breaking it. These were places where killing was a way of life. I guess this is how she met the scum bag she ran off with, leaving her four boys. This guy killed a man in 1968 in a bar. The person supposedly spit on and slapped him. He had a lawn mower in his truck that he pawned for two shells and a sawed off shot gun, came back, kicked the bar door open, and shot the man's heart out of his chest while he was eating black eyed peas and rice. They ran off, and eventually settled in Jacksonville, FL, two hours away, raising his sons. They never called or came to see us.

Scars — Chapter 1

My Grandma and Grandpa struggled with providing for us. It wasn't uncommon for my grandparents to go grocery shopping on Friday, and by Monday, we had eaten mostly everything they bought. We ate everything in sight. We would tear up things. I was five weeks old when Grandma got custody of me. In the morning, she would wrap me up in a blanket and carry me across the street to my baby sitter's house, Ms. Gus. She was a sweet lady. When I got old enough to walk to Ms. Gus' house, I would get walked over there by my Grandma, or my aunt or uncle. My Grandma always made sure she sent cookies and sandwich meat and all kinds of goodies with me every day. In the afternoon, I would see my grandparents pull into the yard. That was my signal to go home. I would take off running as fast as I could to see my grandparents. My Grandpa also bought honey buns home for us.

Ms. Gus was a special lady to me. She treated me as if I were her son by watching out for me in my early years. I continued to go to Ms. Gus' house until I was ready to attend kindergarten. The first day of school, riding on that bus with all those strange people had me terrified. I cried all the way to school. Everything seemed to be moving so fast and so many people were there. When the bus stopped, finally arriving at school, I can remember crying and wishing my Grandma was there to help me find my way.

Going to school in my early years wasn't much fun. I was always sad, and did not like to talk. Every morning I got up for school, my Grandma had eggs, grits, sausage, and homemade biscuits on the table waiting. My Grandma was the best. The bus would let me and my two older brothers off about 2 miles from home. Sometimes it would be so hot, it seemed like we could see the heat moving back and forth across that old dirt road we lived on. We walked home every single day. We were six, seven, and eight. Now once we got home, that was when all the fighting and busting holes in the walls would begin. Our next door neighbor lived about 100 yards from our house, and she would tell my Grandma that it sounded like we were tearing the house down. We had a chicken pen in the backyard. I would go in the pen and slap the hens and make them get off the eggs. I loved eggs. One day, I went to the chicken pen to get eggs, and I guess the hen said to herself, "Here he comes. Today is payback!" That hen started pecking my feet as soon as I walked in. I didn't get any eggs that day. There were many days my Grandma came home, and we all got a whipping for fighting and breaking something, or putting holes in the walls. I have apologized to my granny for all the things we put her through growing up.

I am now in the first grade, and school isn't my favorite place. They put me in speech because I didn't talk well, and I stuttered. Often times, I would sit in class and wonder where my mom was, and if she's still living. One great thing was that every day after school, we would play tackle football until it was dark. When we play football, you would've thought we were in the NFL. There was no mercy. If you ran close to a mailbox, someone would knock you into it. Bloody noses and busted lips happened on the regular. This would turn out to be a gift from God later in life. Other kids would laugh at the way I talked. This scarred me for life. If you want to make me mad, make fun of the way I talk! There was an incident recently, where I was helping a friend get his restaurant going, and he made a smart remark about how I talk. He almost got put in a choke hold! Even now at 41 years old, I am not the best speaker, but life's lessons have taught me to keep working to get better at my short comings.

So I'm going to school every day, still no phone calls from our mom. We see our dad every once in a while. My daddy was a very soft spoken, silky black man with soft curly hair. He was about 6'1, 175lbs. He worked three jobs, and he paid his child support. I understand being a father and having responsibility sometimes doesn't allow us to do all the things we need to do, like visiting your kids more. I don't hold that against him, because he was put in a bad situation with my mom leaving us like she did.

We had this one particular aunt who came to pick us up just about every weekend. She was very strict, and everything had its place at her house. She never really cared that much for me. My younger brother was her favorite when he started school and from day one, he was getting into trouble. My Aunt always blamed me for the things he did at school and at home. It seemed like she only allowed me to come around because we were brothers. It really didn't bother me that she liked him more, what bothered me was that she blamed me for everything he did wrong. A couple of weeks after I burned my foot, we went to her house to spend the night. I was hopping on one leg because of my burned foot. My younger brother and I were playing up the street with a kid in the neighborhood. They got into a scuffle. I was sitting on the embankment watching the whole fight. So the kid ran up on his porch where his mom was sitting, and started yelling and laughing at my brother. My brother picked up a rock, and threw it at him, hitting him right between the eyes. He had to go to the emergency room. When they returned from the hospital, the kid and his mom came over to our Aunt's house to tell her what happened. After his mom finished her story explaining that my brother threw the rock and hit her son, my Aunt still told her that it had to have been me, because I did things like that all the time. After they left, my brother lied and said I did it, and even after the lady tried to tell my aunt that I had nothing to do with it, I still got the whipping! That was the last time I stayed at her house.

Growing up, teachers and people in general, would assume I was the bully because of my size. Being really dark skinned did not help either. There were several painful incidents in my life that I remember. One of them was when my uncle got married in Orlando, FL, and he and his wife had arranged for the kids at the wedding to go to Disney World. But somehow, they didn't have enough tickets for everyone to go, or maybe there were enough tickets, just none for me and my brothers. So they decided that they would send me and my brothers back to Tallahassee with our uncle. I can remember crying, and looking out of the window as we drove off. Every adult and child standing there began to get smaller and smaller. Soon we cried ourselves to sleep. This is another incident that has stuck with me all my life and I promised myself that nobody would ever treat my kids like we were treated.

Another time I remember I had come home from school, it was raining, and me and my brothers were playing. One of my Uncles came over, and the first thing he said when he stepped in the door was, "I wish I could hit you over the head with this couch!" It was times like those that made me feel like when they looked at me, they hated me or disliked me that much. I was only a kid! I remember thinking many times, if my momma and daddy was around, they wouldn't do the things they do to me. Another time I was at my Aunt and Uncle's house sitting on the couch. My uncle was sitting across the room in a chair. He picked up a two or three foot clay cowboy that my aunt had sitting on her coffee table and threatened to throw it at me. I said, "You ain't gonna throw it!", and he threw it! It hit me square in the forehead, and everybody was laughing so hard at me as I sat there with blood dripping down my face. That was when I decided that when I got older, if somebody did something like this to me, I would tear them limb from limb.

When I turned eleven, it was no more taking anything! The monster was born! I started to wear my emotions and feelings on my sleeves. It didn't help that I already felt like me and my brothers were not wanted by our parents, because if they wanted us, we would be with them. Many times, when kids are growing up, people who are supposed to love them make them grow up faster than they need to by the way that those people treat them. One day, me and my Grandma were in the kitchen together, and I told her that I loved her. She told me to get out of the kitchen. I know my Grandma loves me with all her heart, but she didn't know how to handle me telling her I loved her. Because the word was not used around my house at all, I grew up not being able to use the word love. And God knows I really needed that word in my life. I just didn't realize how much until I reached my mid 30's and early 40's. Growing up and not knowing anything about the word love caused me to feel the need to put up a force field around me and be rough and tough.

I am reaching out to every little ten year old boy trying to let them know that they don't have to let the actions of adults cause them to suffer mentally. As an adult, I was always a person who refused to believe that incidents in my life had mentally affected me. But I have come to realize that it has greatly affected me at forty one years old. These incidents continue to influence me, because it's like a movie playing over and over in my head. Now, with so much abuse and murder of kids today, it continues to remind me of the events in my life. I often wonder to myself if anyone in my family ever looked back at me and my brothers and realized how their actions affected us in our lives. Later in this book, a clearer picture will be painted of how these occurrences changed my life.

I learned about Jesus Christ early in my life, and he has put me to the test, I have put him to the test, and he is real! If you don't think it is possible to be forty one, and have the soul of a seventy year old man, you will have a better understanding of how that can happen throughout this book. I really believe that God gave me a gift of being able to look far down the road in my life. As early as ten years old, there would be times where I could be at a certain place, or be riding through a certain place, and feel like I have been there before. I have been told by many people that I have the soul of an old man. I guess that is an advantage of being raised by my grandparents.

CHAPTER 2: Boot Camp

    I know things got off to a rocky start in my life, but there were also good times. In my neighborhood, everyone was kinfolk in some way or another. There were ten to twelve kids in my hood, and we played all kinds of sports. The road I lived on was a dirt road that was a football, softball, basketball, or any arena for sports. After school, my cousins would always call and ask, "Y'all want to get a game of football started?" They were like brothers to me, and we all loved each other. You had to be really rough to play football with us. I was ten playing with guys that were fifteen, sixteen, and seventeen years old. Later this would make it almost impossible for guys to play with me in high school. One of the greatest memories of my childhood was on Friday nights, when my Uncle Michael would have a football game. He played for my high school, the great Amos P. Godby Cougars! All day in school, it was hard for me to pay attention thinking about my grandma boiling those hotdogs and wrapping them in foil to put in her purse. Our grandparents couldn't afford to feed us at a game. We ate too much and they would have gone broke! This would be the only afternoon that we did not go outside and play in the dirt, the game is tonight!!!!!!! It's funny how my kids Peyton and Jerome III remind me of myself. When they know we are going somewhere that excites them; they will ask one hundred times, "Is it time to go yet?" I was the same way, LOL.

In those early years my Uncle Michael inspired me to want to be a football player. He was very good. He did not allow us to be soft. Now, you have to understand my uncle loved us, but some of his punishments were brutal. He would stack our heads on top of each other, all four, and sit on our heads. He would take a pillow, and put it over our face, and keep it there until we almost passed out. The worst was when he would hit us on our thigh with his fist (getting your thigh busted). For about ten minutes, all we could do was lay there and cry. You could not walk. Michael always spent a lot of time with us, like combing my oldest brother's hair in the morning, telling him to stop all that crying or taking us to his summer job as a camp instructor. Finally, we were on our way to the game, two grownups and four young boys in the cab of a 1972 Chevy truck. It was only about a twenty minute ride, but it felt like hours. When we got within view of the stadium, my heart would start pounding as if I was playing in the game. Who would have known this stadium is the place where I turned almost grown men into boys, some eight years later. Arriving early, we were never late anywhere when we went with our grandparents. We would be the first family to church, sitting outside an hour early. This allowed me to see my Uncle and his team pull up to the stadium with the local sheriff leading the team bus with lights and sirens blaring. One day I will be on that bus! The serious look on their faces walking in a straight line, man I cannot tell you the feeling I got watching them walk through the gate ready to play.

Now the stadium was starting to get crowded with fans, and the band was marching in playing some of my favorite songs. I am fired up! Once the game started, I would watch about a quarter, and then go down just outside the end zone fence and play tackle football with other kids my age. We would use a crushed red and white coca cola cup as a football. When I got the cup, the band would be playing, and I would pretend that I was running a touchdown in the game that was being played on the field. After the game, I would stand by the team bus and give the players five. One day, that will be me! Uncle Michael signed a football scholarship with the University of Florida Gators in Gainesville, FL. I was proud of him, but sad that he was leaving home. He would come back home during the summers and train for the upcoming football season, he ran the block in our neighborhood, once claiming the state troopers gave him a ticket for running to fast…LOL.

I am really growing physically. We are still playing football every day. We still haven't heard anything from our mom, but our dad would come to our grandparent's house and see us. Never did he take us anywhere, maybe out for ice cream or something, or to McDonalds. We loved their hamburgers. That Christmas, two of us got the Pittsburgh Steelers helmets and shoulder pads, and the other two got the Buffalo Bills. On the backside of the house was a grassy area that had hedges on both sides that we called the Coliseum, only the best players were allowed to play on this field. We would play football all day until our grandma called us in for dinner to take our baths. We would be so dirty our bath water would look like mud. Writing this chapter brings a smile to my face, thinking about how much fun it was playing and being with my brothers. These times erased all hurt and pain that I felt, just being with them was all that I needed. I can remember at bedtime we lay two in a bed and talk wondering how it would be if we lived with them. This would be the routine for many years to come; doing everything we could to not be sad and upset.

CHAPTER 3: The Big Buy Out

    I was twelve years old when my mom moved back from Jacksonville, FL to Tallahassee, FL. From the first time I laid eyes on her husband, It was apparent that I didn't like him. He didn't like me either. Something about him made my flesh crawl. I could feel it in my soul. After my mom found a place to live, she wanted us to come over and spend the weekend. My brothers were all for it, but I didn't want to spend the night. Not because of my mom, but because of him. Later on that day, me and my younger brother got into an argument. He said, "I can't believe you don't want to be around your momma!" But he didn't understand, it wasn't her, it was her husband. It was strange to me. It was like I could see straight through him, like a window. Even though I didn't want to go spend the weekend, I went anyway, and they started trying to buy us with little things like candy, and pretty much let us do whatever we wanted. They lived in the South City Projects, and they let us have girls back in the room with the door closed and no supervision. Everything seemed too good to be true, and I kept waiting for the real momma and her husband to show up. By them letting all those things go on, my brothers wanted to go over there every weekend. So I continued to watch the situation, because I could tell by the way he talked, he was very mean and hateful. After spending a couple weekends, they started asking us if we wanted to come and live with them. I thought to myself, hell no, my brothers weren't sold on that idea either. When they would ask us about moving with them, we would just be quiet and not say anything. After there was not an answer, they would say, "Go outside and play." I could tell my mom was disappointed; it was too early to ask us that question. After all, she had been gone for years, and we were trying to get to know her. It was months before they asked us about coming to live with them again.

So my mom moved over to Old Bainbridge Road right next to a grave yard, and that was really creepy. I hated being there at night living next to a grave yard. At times it looked like dead bodies would come walking up to the house. One weekend, we were playing outside, and I guess we were making too much noise, so he started cursing and yelling. That was when I really knew that living with them wasn't the place for me, and that I could not stand him! I wished he would leave town and just let it be our mom and us; as long as he was around I wasn't going to live with my mom. One day, we had been to the summer program at Dade Street Recreation Center, where we would go every summer. Dade Street was located right behind my great grandmother's house. That afternoon, after we came home, we saw on the evening news that a four story church, that was probably eighty-five percent complete, had fallen to the ground. And guess who was in the photograph on the front of the newspaper the next day: my step dad! He was completely covered by steel beams. You could see his legs wrapped around and over other beams. I never wanted to see anyone die, but I was wishing that he would get taken away after that accident and leave our mom for her boys. With him around, it would never be all four of her boys, maybe three. Our mom didn't have a lot of time during all of this, which was understandable, because she was back and forth to the hospital. He spent about six or seven months in the hospital with two broken legs. One was so bad it had to be amputated just below the knee. He had a broken neck, two broken arms, and skull fractures. If you could break it, and still live, he had it broken.

As time continued to pass, my mom started telling us about all this money they would get from the accident and how they could buy us anything we wanted. My brothers jumped on that band wagon, but I didn't. Something still wasn't right. Eight months passed before any money started to appear, but it wasn't settlement money. It was money my step dad was borrowing from his attorney. The attorney knew exactly what and with whom he was dealing with: an uneducated person who had been in prison most of his life and was hungry for money.

The Big Buy Out

He really didn't have the mental capacity to let his accident run its course and let the attorney earn his money. Every chance he got, he was borrowing money. He bought old car after old car, and went down to Frenchtown flashing money with all of the money he borrowed. I guess another three or four months went by, and then came the settlement. Back in those days, it looked as if they had received a million dollars, but it was actually just fifty thousand to him, and ten thousand to my mom. What a shame for a man that had gone through an amputation, multiple surgeries, and all kinds of pain and suffering. The lawyer saw him and my mom coming. They walked away with all the money, and my mom and her husband got crumbs. After receiving the settlement, they bought a three bedroom house in a predominantly white neighborhood, which I must admit, was pretty nice. It had all new furniture and glass everywhere. It almost fooled me, but my love for my grandparents would not let me leave them. I loved them too much, and I couldn't abandon them. When we had nowhere to go, when our mom had forgotten all about us and left town without even saying goodbye to me and my brothers, our grandparents were all we had. My mom leaving me stuck in my heart like a bag of heavy rocks, and by the way, my heart has a permanent crack in it that will never be repaired, and her being married to him wasn't going to allow me to live with her. I will die with this crack in my heart. So after we got to the house and played for a while, they called us in and asked about letting them get custody of us from our grandparents. All kinds of promises were made to us. Of course my brothers agreed to move with them. I still refused by saying nothing at the time. When we went back home, I told my grandparents what was said, and I told my Grandma, "My brothers can't see it, but things will be different when they get custody of them."

My grandmother was broken hearted that my brothers wanted to leave her and live with him and momma. So Christmas came before we went to court, and my mom and her husband bought us bikes. They were ready to punish me for refusing to leave my grandparents, so they bought three stylish Huffy bikes and one big red bus with a basket on the front, like the witch on The Wizard of Oz rode when she took Dorothy's dog away. I cried all day Christmas day! My brothers tried to tell me it wasn't planned but I knew it was, because we all came in the living room at the same time, and I got to one of the huffy bikes first, but my Momma and her husband pointed to the bus and said, "That one is yours Jerome." A few months after Christmas we went to custody court, and my grandmother gave my momma custody of my three brothers and kept custody of me. It felt like my brothers were moving out of town when they would only be a few miles away. A few weeks passed before I went over to their house. Every weekend my mom would take them shopping, and not once did she take me, or buy me anything. That hurt, but not nearly as much as how they treated me when I came to spend the night with them. In no way was I a saint or anything, but my mom and her husband had talked against me so much, that my brothers acted like they hated me also. When I went to their house, they would say things like, "Don't come over here starting trouble!" Then they would always try to fight me, all three of them. It made me feel like they didn't want me there, so I would call my granddaddy to come and get me. My grandparents would tell me not to go over to their house, but I couldn't because my brothers were all I knew, and I loved and missed them.

My stepdad would mistreat me, and my mom wouldn't say a word! She would turn a deaf ear and a blind eye to the situation. There were many times they went on family trips, and not one time did they invite me to go. One particular time, they were leaving to go to West Palm Beach, FL, and I was walking in front of Dade Street Recreation Center and they drove by. My mom saw me so they stopped. While my mom talked to me, my brothers wouldn't even speak to me. They barely looked at me. I walked away with my head down. It was hard to believe that those three boys I had so much in common with would treat me the way they did that day. The biggest incident that hurt me the most was one day, when me and my brother, who's one year older than me, got into a fight. When my momma and her husband came home, my brother told them that I broke a picture of his girlfriend, and immediately, my mom and her husband told me to get my things so he could take me home. I started crying because I couldn't believe my mom was doing that. I expected that from him, but not her. I got my things and put them in a pillow case, and he drove me home. Well, he dropped me off about a half mile from my house and told me to walk the rest of the way! There were many other times I tried to go over to their house and stay, but it seemed like he and my mom just didn't care for me. Even after they mistreated me every time I went over there, I still loved and missed my brothers, so from time to time, I would go back over there.

After about two years, all the good times started to fade. There were no more shopping sprees on the weekends, and the out of town trips stopped. My mom's husband had bought a very pretty customized van and a 1968 Buick Electra and had it restored. It was white with blue leather interior. Everybody loved that car. He started his own business called *Junking*. He bought old cars, scrap metal, and things a normal person would call junk, and then resold it. He actually made a lot of money doing it. One day he made a deal with a white guy in a small town outside of Tallahassee called Havana, Florida. Whatever deal it was, he let the guy hold the car title to the Buick. It was a beautiful Saturday, and me and my younger brother were playing football in the ditch. This white guy was walking up the street and he came in the yard. My momma and her husband were both outside. The white guy had a piece of paper in his hand and acted as if he was reading information off of the paper. He said, "I heard you had a 1968 Buick for sale." My mom's husband said, "Yea, if the price is right." So the guys asked to test drive the car. My mom's husband said, "Go ahead." He threw him the keys, and the guy went around the corner. The car had pipes coming out of the back called duals. They were loud when you pressed the gas. That was all we could hear at the house.

    Now this is a weekend I wish me and my cousin weren't over to their house. I saw everyone loading up in the van, but me and my younger brother kept playing football in the ditch. When my mom's husband said, "Y'all come and go with us," we had no idea where we were going until we pulled up in front of a white house with a mechanic garage connected to it. We got out of the van, and my mom's husband and my step brothers walked up on the porch. The owner told them to come in where they could talk. The whole idea behind that statement was to get them in the house, shoot and kill them, so they could then tell the police that they were trying to do bodily harm to them in their house. After they entered the house, there was a lot of noise as if furniture was being broken. My mom's husband and my step brothers started backing out of the house, the whole time punching and cursing. Then everybody started fighting. Men were coming out of the garage with tools, swinging them at everyone. I took cover beside an old junk car located in front of the house. Then the owner shouted, "Honey, get the gun!" Somehow, my little cousin, who was about three at the time, was sitting at the front door, and his wife came out and pointed the gun right at her head, then lifted the gun and shot my mom's husband in the elbow, hitting an artery. Blood was spraying everywhere. Somehow, we all got in the van, and headed for the hospital. Everybody was crying, and my mom's husband went unconscious. Blood was about an inch thick on the floor mat and it had chilled like Jell-O. We were racing down Highway 27 to the hospital. His eyes had rolled back in his head. I thought he was dead. When we made it to the hospital, the doctor came out after they got him in the back, and said if we would have had to drive a half a block more to get him to the hospital, he wouldn't have made it. I couldn't wait to get home and see my grandparents. I thought I was never going to see them again.

CHAPTER 4: Young Boy Doing Man Things

My mom and her husband started to fall on hard times. All of a sudden out of the blue, they sold that beautiful house. After selling the house they moved over to Calloway Street located in the black neighborhood. It was a decent place to live, but the house was really small compared to the house they had lived in before. They may have lived on Calloway Street a year or two, and then moved to Sunnyside Drive where my nightmare would begin. This is where I met the girl from hell!

When my mom moved to Sunnyside Drive, they treated me a little better at times, but my mom's husband never liked me. I guess it had to do with the fact that every time my name was mentioned, he thought about my dad. I was a kid and hadn't done anything to him. How could he dislike a child that much? I had started to spend a lot of time at my mom's house even though he didn't like me. There were many things to witness at my mom's. There were things that young kids should never see. During this time of my life, my brothers and I were starting to go girl crazy, among other things. We had begun to hang out in the streets running behind girls, girls, and more girls. We were pretty popular in Tallahassee; they called us the Martin brothers. We all had many friends, but we had two guys that we were really cool with. It seemed so easy with the girls around my way, or they just liked me that much. I learned many things from my two older brothers. Me and my younger brother were in training, to say the least. There were parties all over the place we would go to. Dade Street Recreation Center and Walker Ford Recreation Center were a couple of places that had parties. When we would get to the parties, there would be girls waiting on us. We would divide up dancing and talking to them. Many times we would have been drinking before the party, and during, or both. There were times when a girl might turn me down, but there weren't many, and to think, I wasn't good in football yet! Isn't that something?! The biggest problem with all of this is that nobody ever sat me and my brothers down and talked about the birds and the bees. I would end up paying for the fact of not being taught. It's amazing to me now that we were running wild, and nobody felt the need to sit us down and talk to us. I guess this is another example of nobody really caring about what happened.

There was a party at a friend's house. This particular party would give me eighteen years of hell! I remember the night we were getting dressed, smoking and drinking like always. After arriving at the party, we made a grand entrance and started mingling with everyone. We were really having a good time dancing and running in and out of the party. Later that night, I noticed this short dark skinned girl sitting on the sofa. She seemed rather shy, like her mom might not let her get out much, so I slid over and asked her name. She answered me and we started talking. When the party was over, we started walking home. I asked her where she lived, and what do you know, she lived down the path that went through my mom's yard, so I walked her home. The next day I went over to her house, and the strangest thing happened. Her mom was sitting on the sofa, I spoke to her, and she asked my name and a few other questions. The new girl was in the bedroom, so she called me to her room. I was really confused. It was hard to believe that her mom allowed boys in her daughter's room, but she didn't care.

Over the next few weeks, I continued to go over to her house after school. She was older than me. I was still in middle school at Griffin Middle, and she was at Florida A&M High. The girls at that school thought they were all of that and a bag of chips, but yours truly had caught one of them, and what a bad catch it turned out to be; it was something like a bad dream. We became boyfriend and girlfriend and started doing grown people things, which soon produced our twin sons. The hardest part of the situation to believe, was that I was in the eighth grade, and I had gotten a girl pregnant with twins, wow! Once she was pregnant, we started to grow apart because of our families. My family was saying that the babies weren't mine, because I was too young. Her family was saying different, and they would be right. The next nine months were rocky. There was a lot of things said from both sides, and through all of this, we very seldom talked. One night, the phone rang. It was my oldest brother. He called to tell me she had twins, and they were waiting on the third child. My jaw dropped open as if Mike Tyson had hit me in it. That was the worst joke he ever played on me. It was hard to believe I was in the eighth grade with a set of twins in the world. I must clarify one thing though, and that is not being sorry that my sons were born. I just wish it would have been much later in life.

I feel very responsible for the way their lives turned out. Even though we were young when the kids were born, there still was a chance for them to have a productive life, but when the mom only says negative things about their dad and the people who are willing to be a part of the kid's lives, it's hard for that to happen. It takes a collective effort to raise children and that is what should have happened with my twins. After the twins were born, their mom started wanting to put me up for child support. Every man should provide financially for his children, but my situation was very different from your typical situation. I was fourteen and wasn't old enough to legally provide for them. Even though I wasn't old enough to support them, my grandparents were willing to support the children until I became of age to do so. Her whole family was child support and welfare professionals, so she decided to put me on child support. I didn't go to court until tenth grade. The judge said that he would not require me to pay child support until I finished high school. She was furious! It had gotten to the point where the support wasn't the issue. She just wanted to hurt me. There weren't many times that my twins were around me, because I didn't see her much, and she moved around a lot.

As my boys started getting older, she started to talk against me and give them a negative attitude towards me and my grandparents. Realizing the situation I had gotten myself into, football started to be my central focus, because I knew that it would be my way to take care of my sons. While I was in college, my sons began to spend a lot of time at my house with my grandparents. My grandmother had them going to church and doing positive things. All of a sudden, their mom stopped letting them come over to my house. That proved to be a crucial mistake. Their mom started getting involved with all kinds of different guys: ex-cons, drug dealers, and an assortment of different characters. There were times we would talk, and she actually bragged and boasted about these guys. What a shame, because they represented nothing but negativity around my sons. This is why I regret having them so young and with her! Her mothering skills weren't up to par. She upheld our sons when they were wrong, and there was no discipline at all! But the discipline she didn't give, the correctional system did! One of the biggest reasons things turned out bad for them was the fact that I wasn't around.

I take full responsibility. As my sons became older, they started skipping school, getting arrested, and all she had was excuses and she blamed all their faults on other people. It would soon end. I can remember their mom telling me about all the people in the streets that loved the twins. She was so naïve that she didn't realize that all they were after was her, because she was so easy to get involved with. I should have been there for my boys, like I am here for my three children now. These are the negatives associated with having children young: babies having babies.

CHAPTER 5: Learning Life's Lessons

After the word had spread about me having twins, the action with the girls slowed down, but it never stopped. I had reached the ninth grade, and things were the same for me, as they were for a forty year old man: going to child support court, having paternity tests, and trying to stay mentally focused. I was playing football on the junior varsity team. Soon I would be moved up to the varsity football team. The coach I had on my junior varsity team said I was a bully because the white guys were being dominated by me every practice. He didn't know that the situation with my twins was weighing heavily on my mind. There was grown-man pressure on me as a fourteen year old ninth grader, and man, what pressure! My ninth grade year would pass, and I entered the tenth grade. It wasn't much different than the ninth grade, except that my football talents were really starting to develop and be noticed by my coaches.

Even though there wasn't much interest in my academics at home, I wanted to get out of the basic classes and try the college prep classes. There was just one problem: my 9th grade English teacher. At the end of the year, it was time to decide on my courses for the next year. She told me I wasn't college prep material. There was no problem with me doing the work; it was a matter of me applying myself. So she put me in the basic English class. I went home and told my grandma, but she just over looked what I told her. This would change my life in such a negative way and damage me forever. My grandma did not want to get involved. You see, she was my 9th grade teacher's maid, and she thought she would get fired if she addressed the situation. The teachers judged me because I was big and dark skinned and not light skinned with curly hair. I was still in some college prep courses, such as Spanish, even though my speaking still wasn't the best. I was trying and doing pretty well, but she killed all my confidence and drive. Looking back on the situation, it shouldn't have been that easy to discourage me, but it's not like I grew up with people building me up academically, or in life period. She made me doubt myself. It would start to contribute to the angry feelings I had been having since I was a young boy: people taking me for granted and never expecting anything good out of me.

The angry feelings started to show on the football field and in the streets. I would be getting ready for a game and start crying uncontrollably, because all I knew was that I was going to get respect on that football field. I was going to show them, and what a show of aggression it would turn out to be! I would feel pure hate and violence on the field. I was on a mission to destroy everything in my way. I had started to fight every weekend, but never in school. By this time, I had been painted a thug by people all over town. So I decided to thug it out, on and off the field. I really didn't know who was actually saying those things, but all I knew was that their sons would pay the ultimate price on the football field. The thing I didn't realize at the time, was that those feelings would continue to grow like a raging fire as time passed. The comments got worse and very ugly. It seemed like the better I played, the meaner and nastier the comments got. Many of them were just vicious attacks on a sixteen year old kid; maybe because I looked like a man, they forgot I was a kid. Every time a comment was made, I played that much harder, coming faster and stronger with every tackle and every punch off of the field. At times, on the field, I would move in on a tackle, and I would be biting down on my mouth piece about to bite a hole through it, feeling so much hate and anger. Some of my anger was toward myself, knowing I had twins. I could see that my life, and my twin's lives, would be difficult if I didn't make it in football.

I entered my junior year as an up and coming football player. There was some interest from some colleges. There were many interesting moments of my junior year, but two stick out in my mind more than others. One was when my oldest brother was playing for a cross town rival, Tallahassee Rickards High School. My brother, who's one year older than me, played with me for Godby High School. My oldest brother was a wingback, my other brother was a strong safety, and I was a middle linebacker. The way we played against each other, you would have thought we weren't brothers at all. I must admit, my oldest brother was a really good wingback. He rushed for eleven hundred yards that year, but me and my other brother were out for blood. Every time he touched that football, we came harder and harder. No matter how hard we hit him, he ran harder the next play. That was our brother, and he was no punk. We kept coming at all costs. That Friday night is near and dear to my heart. It gives me a great memory of the game that we played that night. I guess we all played with anger and hurt in our hearts. People didn't expect much out of us, but we could play football, and they couldn't take that away from us. My uncles and aunts told us that on the radio all they talked about was the way those three Martin brothers were playing. I could remember being in the huddle with my brother and both of us saying, "Come on, we are going to get him this next play."There was one other player on our defense that I must mention, the free safety. I will tell you more about him later.

SCARS — CHAPTER 5

My junior year would come to an end, and there were a lot of street situations, such as guys sending messages to me telling me they better not catch me in certain parts of town or at certain parties. Of course, me being who I am, that didn't stop me, because they didn't scare me. So I found myself fighting every weekend. Some of the people I was fighting went to my school, but most went to the other schools. Even though some of them went to my school, I wouldn't fight in school because I would get suspended, and then I couldn't play football. But on the weekend, I would put it on them in a bad way. I refused to be told when and where I could go by anyone.

During the summer, I got arrested involving a very serious crime that would threaten my freedom and football forever. I went to jail with my younger brother on a couple of very serious felony charges, which could have carried capital punishment: electric chair. I went to jail for the first time for being involved in a gang fight where my best friend got hit in the head with an axe handle and another guy got his ear knocked off. After the fight we committed a very serious crime against the guy who split my friend's head open, and he was on our football team. The next day, I went over to my friend's house to check on him. While there, his mom asked us to go and get a loaf of bread from the store. On the way back, we pass a Tallahassee police car.

As we pass, I look in the side mirror, and he does a u-turn in the middle of the street. I immediately think about the night before. He follows us for a short distance in the projects, and then he turns his lights on. A few minutes later, about six or seven other police cars show up. They arrest me and let my friend go because he had about 100 stitches in his head from the fight. They take me to the Tallahassee police station where they try and interrogate me, nice try. Later that night, around eleven o'clock, they decide it was time to take me to jail.

They put me in hand cuffs, and we leave for the juvenile detention center, but on the way, the officer opens the glass window to talk to me about what happened. He was trying to get some answers about what had happened the night before, nice try again. I told him there was nothing to talk about, so he changes subjects and asks me if we went to get my little brother, would he fight or come quietly. I told him that he wouldn't resist. Me being me, I had a bigger plan in mind. If he went and got my little brother, it would give me time to talk to him because we were in deep do-do, and if he didn't listen, we were going down the creek without a paddle. We pull up in front of my mom's house, and my little brother looks out of the blinds and walks outside. The officer immediately places him under arrest, but I didn't have a shirt on, so I asked the officer if I could get a shirt, and he said yes. I got out of the car and went to the door and shouted up stairs, "Momma, they taking Dwayne!" She came down stairs cursing at the officer. She started crying, and when they hand cuffed us together, I told momma, "We will be alright, go back in the house." He put us in the car and pulled off. My brother started crying. A tear or two fell from my eye seeing him cry. He kept saying that they told him if he came back, they would send him off to a reformatory school.

We were about six or seven blocks away from the juvenile center, and I said to him, "If you never hear anything else in life, hear this; tell them you stayed in the car!" If they were sending anyone anywhere, it was going to be me, and he listened. We pulled up to the juvenile detention center. My brother was still crying. I was willing to man up for both of us. The officer walked us in hand cuffed together. After booking and processing us into the facility, they put us in a cell directly across from each other. That night, we just stood and looked at each other through the peep window. The next morning, we came out to eat breakfast. When they opened the cell, I grabbed my little brother by his hand, letting him know nobody was going to bother him.

The feelings that summer were enormous, knowing it could've all been over at the tap of the judge's gavel. This is a point in my life that I thought would be the true turning point, turning away from the fighting and thuggery. How wrong I would turn out to be. Later that morning, we went to court, and they let me out, and he had to stay. That was the first time I would cry, having to leave my little brother.

Had someone died in that situation, it would have been a capital crime which automatically carried the death penalty. I would have been seventeen on death row, and my brother would have been fifteen on death row. I can remember my life at seventeen being in limbo.

CHAPTER 6: Gone Too Soon

    The summer would come to an end, and I just narrowly escaped what could have been the most damaging blow in my life. I entered fall football practice like a wild dog just let out of his cage after years of captivity. With the case I had gone through during the summer, my life flashed before my eyes. My mind was set on not doing anymore fighting or getting in trouble, but that was easier said than done. The more I tried to get away from the fighting, the more I got confronted by guys around town. There was no way anybody was going to just punk me out, so the fighting started all over again. I was dominating on the football field. My first game, I had eight solo tackles, five assists, three or four quarterback sacks, caught a fifty eight yard touchdown, and it only got better! I was so superior on the football field that the media started saying I was a grown man playing with boys. The college scouts started to show real interest.

    I had been practicing for years on the dirt road called Gearhart Road, and I took full advantage of this year. Before every game, I would go into my normal routine of crying like a baby uncontrollably. It was the passion that I had for the game of football, but most of all, it was the hate and anger that I felt for life and all the people who ever said anything negative about me.

It's my senior year, and I know it's either play hell'of-a football, or stay in Tallahassee and go to prison or get killed. So I started balling that much harder! The weekend fights started getting worse, because the guys around town were feeling their manhood and were taking defeat more serious than ever before. One weekend, I got into a fight with a guy from Lincoln High School across town on Florida A&M's campus at Howard Hall, which put ugly memories in my life forever. I never really knew what the fight was all about, except that he played fullback for Lincoln, and he wasn't any good. And I let him know that every time I tackled him! It was months later, but I came to realize that he carried the things I said to him on the football field, off of the football field. One night, on Rollins Street, two girls I went to school with had a party, and the same guy that I had the fight with showed up. The girls refused to let him in. Before the party started, me and my friend, the free safety that I mentioned earlier, and a few more guys went to Mike's Beer Barn and bought a case of Ice Man Malt Liquor and returned to the party. We parked down the street from the house. At the time, I was driving a canary yellow 1974 Monte Carlo. The party started, so me and my friend grabbed a few beers a piece, and walked up the street to the party. We decided to sit across the street on the embankment on the side of the cars to finish the beers we were drinking. After sitting there for a while, here came several guys who went to Lincoln High School from across town. We were sitting behind the cars watching them try and enter the party. They couldn't get in, so they decided to leave. About the same time, my friend asked me to go get a few more beers. I said, "Let them leave and I will." When I thought they were gone, I started walking down to my car, and then one of the guys jumped out and hit me in the chest. I thought he punched me, but he had actually stabbed me in the chest right beside my heart! At the time, I didn't realize he had stabbed me, because it was three guys with knives against me, but the will to live, and the street thug would soon appear. Somehow we ended up in a ditch about six feet deep. The guy I was fighting, I was choking. His eyes were rolling back in his head like a person going to meet his maker. At that point, those were my intentions. I felt a rip in my rib cage, which turned out to be one of his buddies stabbing me in the ribs. I was fighting so hard, I never really felt the pain of the stab wounds. After fighting for what seemed like an eternity, I jumped out of the ditch and ran about ten or twenty yards and stopped. I noticed it was hard for me to breathe, so I looked down and blood was squirting all over my chest and pants. I had on all white! It looked like a scene right out of

Friday the 13th. I began to go to people standing by their cars asking them to help and give me a ride to the hospital, but they all walked off, except for Fleabag and my buddy Roger. Fleabag lifted me up on the trunk of Roger's brand new 1983 Buick Regal and told me not to move. He ran to get Roger from the party. When they started running back to the car, I began to wonder if I would make it through this situation; things were looking pretty grim for me. They threw me in the car and took off with me lying in Fleabag's lap. He kept telling me to hold on a little longer. Then all I remember was being in a tunnel, and there was a very bright light at the end. I was moving toward that light at the speed of sound. I can remember twisting and turning and having my arms stretched out in front of me trying to stop myself from reaching that bright light at the end of the tunnel. Briefly my eyes opened, and all kinds of doctors and nurses all around me were ripping my clothes off inserting tubes. I passed out again. A day or two later, I woke up in the hospital seeing my aunt and my grandmother sitting in the chairs in the room. One of the first things my aunt said to me was, "You know your friend is dead don't you?" I just started crying uncontrollably.

I got out of the hospital a few days later, and the only thing I had to look forward to was going to prom. I remember wearing a white tuxedo and pink bow tie and cummerbund, with my stab wounds still fresh. My chest was swollen with scar tissue and old blood, with a large bandage dressing under my shirt. Then out of nowhere, I looked down at my chest, and there is blood all over my tuxedo. I had to leave. I reached the car and started to cry, not because of the blood, but because I knew the next day was my friend's funeral. All I could see was my buddy laying in that parking lot covered with a white sheet, with blood running down the hill like a person was washing a car. Would I make it through this situation? Only God in heaven knows. I still remember the song *Smile*, by Angela Winbush playing on the radio, which is hard to listen to now. I cried all the way to his funeral, and all the way back. Still to this day, I think about it, as if it was yesterday. I have been to many funerals, but that was probably the second hardest funeral I have ever attended. My older brother's funeral was the hardest.

How does a person deal with so much hurt and pain at eighteen years of age? This would be another one of those growing moments, even if I didn't realize it at the time. Life is a growing process, from the time of conception, until you pass away. This is one incident in a long line of incidents. I would now finish my senior year with a bigger black cloud than ever before over my head. My survival of two major incidents had me really wondering just how long God would let me live. One thing for sure was that I needed to leave Tallahassee and stay gone for a long time. Everything in my life was moving so fast, and there was no way to slow things down. I signed a football scholarship with North Alabama University in Florence, AL. It wasn't where I wanted to go, but my grades kept me from signing with Florida State, Ohio State, and all the other major colleges that were recruiting me. There were a lot of them! I spent the spring of my senior year recovering from my stab wounds and realizing that it was time to leave Tallahassee in August. As I finished my senior year, it was obvious that everyone was afraid of me, not physically, but feeling like where ever I was, death and destruction followed. During this time in my life, there was an inner struggle. It was like a highway, a part goes right and the other goes left. One of the roads was going to lead to death or prison, the other to life. Which road would I take: life or death?

CHAPTER 7: Sam & Ola Mae Dupree

In January 1987, I left for Coffeyville, KS on a 6:00a.m.flight. It made me nervous, because I had not really been away from my grandparents, except to play high school football games. I really loved Sam and Ola Mae Dupree. My grandparents gave all they had to allow their grandson a chance to succeed at life, even though there were people in our family who thought they were wasting precious time and money on someone who wouldn't amount to much anyway. I can remember looking out the window when my plane started to taxi away from the gate, and my grandparents began to get smaller and smaller. With Janet Jackson's *Let's Wait Awhile* playing in my walkman, tears started flowing. I would miss my ole man and granny. The tears would eventually lull me to sleep. When I woke up we were over the Tulsa Oklahoma Airport. All I could see was snow everywhere. It was time to grow up and man up! My plane finally landed. Being a Florida boy, all the snow was new to me. After walking up to the terminal, I met a guy who would become one of my best friends and roommate. He also happened to be the son of my junior college coach.

We loaded up in a white prison van and started the two and a half hour trip to Coffeyville, KS. Riding along the road, there were mini oil wells, buffalo, and every once in a while, a house sitting so far across the field you needed binoculars to see it. All I knew on that ride was that I had a lot to prove to myself, all the people back home, and to my twins. I wanted to show them that their dad would be able to provide for them. Finally, we arrive on campus, get unpacked, and start meeting some of the other football players. Kansas was a brutally cold place. It was a small one horse town. The campus was only four buildings, and everything closed around 9:00pm. If you needed to go shopping, the only choice was Wal-Mart. This was a big time JUCO (Junior College) where you pretty much had to be placed by a major division 1 school to attend and play football. I was placed at Coffeyville by the Florida State Seminoles who I had planned to sign with after Juco, but sometimes our plan is not God's plan! There are two important things that Coffeyville provided: my associate's degree and the chance to grow up and learn survival skills.

That night, I attended a basketball game and talked briefly with the head football coach, who turned out to be one of the biggest liars I have ever met, but so what. I am all in on this one. This is the last chance school for guys like me. You had to either finish or go home and hang out in the streets. I spent the next year and a half in Coffeyville with the dream of graduating and going on to play division 1 football, but along the way, things started to become clearer. There was more to this journey than playing division 1 football. The first semester went really well. I was in the best physical shape of my life: 228 pounds with a 28 inch waist. I had met many new friends from all over the country. My granny was proud of me. It was almost spring break, and I couldn't wait to see my ole man, granny, and my girlfriend since the 10th grade. That feeling of seeing my grandparents was incredible. Remember, I hadn't been away from them ever in life. I enjoyed spring break.

I flew back to Tulsa, OK and had to get back to campus the best way I could, because the coaches no longer picked me up. The great thing about going back was that there was only one month left before summer break. Before I realized it, the summer break had come and gone, and it was time to go back for fall football. The schedule at Coffeyville was similar to military style life. We had to be everywhere at a certain time, and if you were late, you paid dearly. There were many foreign exchange students that attended the college, and we all ate in the student center, which only prepared a certain amount of food each day. Many times, we came in from football practice late, and all the food, except for cereal and salad, would be gone. If you didn't have any money, or a local girl, you went to bed hungry. On Saturday's, we ate twice: once at noon and at 4:00pm. Sunday, we ate at noon, and for the rest of the day, you were on your own. Monday morning, the cafeteria line would be a mile and half long at 6:00am, when it didn't open until 7:00am. We ate like prisoners: big blocks of powdered eggs and half-done bacon. The food wasn't fit for any human, but this was the price I had to pay for not dedicating myself to my grades in high school. The head coach taught me my first valuable lesson: not to trust most football coaches. This man had driven from Kansas to Florida to get me to come to his school. After playing one season for him, I learned that he wasn't a real big fan of guys from Florida. He loved the football player from Florida, but hated the person from Florida. He said that guys from Florida were nothing but booze drinkers and women chasers. I found out later that he told Florida State that I failed a drug test and that never happened! The great thing about this experience was that I didn't need to prove myself playing football. I needed to get my academics together and grow up. So after the season, he stopped paying for my school and blocked me from going back to Florida State to prove his point. This was my final semester at Coffeyville.

I took a trip to visit Western Kentucky University and on the return trip back to Coffeyville, I caught strep throat. After making it back to campus very sick, I laid in the bed with a 104 degree temperature for a week until my roommate's girlfriend, who was a nurse, got me out of bed and drove me to the hospital. The doctor told me if I had laid there a couple more days, there could have been brain damage. Though it got really hard, I had to finish what I started. There was a better place for me, and now that I am older, I see that Tallahassee wasn't where God wanted me to be. God provided me with four precious gifts that will forever change my life later in my journey. Sometimes, I would look up in the sky while practicing football and it seemed as if I could see my grandparents back home in Tallahassee: my grandma taking in the clothes from the line she would hang them on to dry and my grandpa plowing the 10 acre field that he farmed every year with his mule. There were so many emotions that were experienced in Coffeyville from my great grandmother dying, to home sickness, and my high school girlfriend breakup, but through it all, I was determined to stick it out.

Quitting wasn't an option. I learned that there was so much more to life than football. For most players, the game is less than 1% of their lives. All I knew was that all those people who told my grandparents that they were crazy for sticking with me would not be able to laugh at them and say, "I told you he would mess it all up." People in my family didn't know that I knew the things that they said about me that made my granny cry. My love for my grandparents runs so deep; if someone messed with them, I wouldn't be responsible for what would happen to that person.

The head coach had done all he could do to stop me from signing with another university. So one day, in my last semester, my high school coach calls my dorm and tells me that the Florida Gators want me to come and play for them. But there's one problem: they don't have any more scholarships available. They tell me that I will be labeled as a walk on, but I wouldn't have to pay anything. All I could think about was, "What if something goes wrong?" My grandparents didn't have any money to pay for my school. Remember, I just got finished with a shady coach, and I wasn't trusting coaches at that time! The end of the semester was fast approaching, and I was graduating from Coffeyville with a 2.8 GPA. I had taken 21 hours my last semester. I was set to sign my scholarship with Florida A&M University, an HBCU (Historically Black Colleges & Universities) in my hometown of Tallahassee, FL. The next day after arriving home, I report to the football office, and of course, they don't have the scholarship ready for me to sign. This is in May. I wait around until the latter part of June, and still no scholarship. There are other schools calling and wanting to sign me, so I told five schools to send me their scholarships, and the first one I received was who I was going to sign with. It ended up being Western Kentucky University. If I can leave parents with one piece of advice, it would be do not put your faith in any coach! The next day, I was on a greyhound bus headed to Bowling Green, KY to play for the Hilltoppers. By the way, what is a Hilltopper?

There's a new sheriff in town, and he has a chip on his shoulder. Some of the upper classmen reporting for fall thought I was a freshman, and they would soon learn that I came to show them exactly what it meant to play "pissed off." My summer roommate was Chandler Wallace, who was a cool dude. We hit it off pretty well. It was the place for me. Bowling Green was just large enough to allow my continued growth from boy to man. A person's age does not dictate when you are grown. That happens when you learn to deal with life's adverse situations.

One summer July day, my life would change for the better. I met my beautiful wife! There were a few football players in summer school that summer, and one day, they decided to go to the mall. I wanted to go to the liquor store, but they insisted on going to the mall, not knowing this trip would change my life in more than just one way. We all came walking down the middle of the mall, and behind a merchandising table at Berman's Leather is a pretty slim girl. I am really not interested at the time. I want to go to the liquor store. After some of my friends try their luck, I decide to go over to the table and see what I could do; it works, and she gave me her number. We finally decide to leave and head to one of my favorite places, the package store. I am back at my dorm around 5:30 or 6:00. She told me that she got off and would be home around 8:00pm. I would never tell, but I was excited to call her. She was very pretty and nice. We start talking every day. She attends my university, and we are now an item. I really care about her a lot, and my feelings are growing every day for her. We continue to date, and we are in love with each other. She really looks out for me in more than one or two ways: every game she makes sure I am dressed to the tee and makes sure I eat every night at her house. Her mom would cook a Thanksgiving type meal every day! I really adored her mom. She was a really strong black woman who was the driving force behind her family! My mother-in-law did not care that I was supposed to be this superstar football player; she told me exactly what was on her mind. I respected her so much. My kids got cheated because they never got to know their grandmother, Virginia Earl Carver,

SCARS — CHAPTER 7

one hell of a woman! Be careful in life. You never know where your final destination will be. I never knew that pretty little girl behind that table would be my wife and the mother of three of my kids. There will be many hurdles to cross on our way to marriage, but I am glad we are making the journey together.

In 1990, the Green Bay Packers pick me in the 10th round of the NFL Draft! I can't describe the feeling I had when they called me and said they were getting ready to draft me with their next selection. The return phone call was better than the initial phone call! While getting drafted was great, there were so many emotions running through my mind. I wanted to do some nice things for my grandparents who love me for no reason at all, except for the fact that they love me. I want to take care of my twin boys, and of course my future wife, Nicole. Lord this is my chance to finally get out of poverty. I never felt like I was living in poverty, but the truth was, I was poor, according to society.

Now let's go back to shortly before the draft. My life seemed as if it was crumbling right before my eyes. One day after class, I was on my way to the football stadium for spring football practice. When I walked in the front door leading to the locker room, Coach Jack Harbaugh was standing in the lobby of his office, and I looked him in his eyes. Immediately, I realized something was very wrong. So I dropped my head and kept walking, but he called me over to his office and told me that the injury I sustained to my left ankle when I was a freshman at North Alabama wasn't documented correctly. The NCAA denied my final year of eligibility. In other words, my college career was over! What a crushing blow when a pro scout from Tampa Bay had me projected, at the latest, a 4th round pick the following year. Those words he spoke cut through my heart like a bow and arrow. Now the path to my life is no longer clear. It is very cloudy, but it gets much worse! I immediately leave the football stadium and start down the side walk down to my dorm room. That was very hard: walking down the sidewalk being denied the opportunity to play football, the sport that I loved. After getting to my room, I turned on the TV. Oprah was on and Johnny Gill, an R&B singer, was singing; then it hit me, call Nicole!

    I picked up the phone and called, thinking she had made it home from class. It never dawned on me that I didn't see her on campus. We met every day after class, and she would go to my room until I had to report for football practice. Receiving the bad news of not playing college football anymore took away all of my normal thoughts. Anyway, I got her nephew Byron on the phone, and he says, "Tank is in the hospital, she was in a car accident," (Tank is her nickname). I said, "Man stop playing." He said, "I'm not joking!" I immediately jumped up and ran from my dorm all the way up to the top of campus, where the football team was having a team meeting. I burst in the meeting and told my roommate that I needed his car keys. I then ran all the way back past my dorm, about a mile and a half without stopping, to where his car was parked, jumped in the car, and headed for the hospital. I finally got there. As I was walking through the hospital asking staff where she was, I saw her parents in the dining area. So I asked how she was doing and everyone gave this "not good" look. We sat there for a while, and then the doctor came in and said, "She had internal bleeding, and we can't stop it. If it doesn't stop within the next couple hours, she will die. We have a team of doctors that we're consulting with from Nashville, TN, and hopefully we will figure it out." Could my day and life turn this bad in just a few hours? We waited about another two hours, and the doctor came back to the waiting area with great news! The lord stopped the bleeding. What a blessing! Maybe an hour later I returned to the dorm.

Everyone always hung out in my room. When I got in my room, my roommate, and one of my best friends, Russell Foster, asked questions about her condition, and I broke down in an uncontrollable cry. This wasn't like me to cry in front of friends or people period. But I loved her. The remainder of my weekend would be spent going back and forth to the hospital. The next day, Saturday, I was able to see her. What a horrifying sight: tubes and IV lines running everywhere. She is sedated heavily. I just know I am not leaving her side. The weekend passes, and the next week I try to continue going to class, but the thought of her in the hospital would not let me go, so I started going to the hospital every day, leaving only to work out for NFL scouts. I only needed 3 hours and an internship to graduate with a degree in Physical Education with a minor in Recreation, but for her, I would risk it all! Seeing her like that every day made me feel the real need to make a NFL team to take care of her.

The scouts started coming two or three every day. I remember the first scout was from the Seattle Seahawks on a cold rainy Saturday. Nicole had bought me a gold necklace that I wore at all times. I would get down to run the 40 yard dash, giving the necklace a kiss, and think of her. Tears would come to my eyes, and then out the hole I came with the song *Secret Garden* by Al B. Sure, El DeBarge, and Barry White playing in my head, smoking past the NFL scouts in 4.53, 4.51, and 4.50.

Scars — Chapter 7

For a 222 pound strong safety, that is blazing! This continued for about two months coming up to the 1990 NFL football draft, which would have players such as Emmitt Smith picked in the draft. Life is really confusing to me at this point. My girlfriend is in the hospital, I have quit going to school, and football isn't a given at this point. I guess this is why through all the ups and downs of 18 years of marriage, God continues to bless us and keep us together, because I threw it all up in the air to be by her side. After about two months in the hospital, she gets to go home, which is the first day of the NFL draft.

I knew if a team would draft me, it wouldn't be on the first day, so I go to see her after the first five rounds of the draft. I was glad to see her but feeling a little down wondering if I would be drafted the next day. The next day came, and I stayed in my room all day waiting for that call from a NFL team. That afternoon, the Green Bay Packers called, and drafted me in the 10th round. What a relief! My baby was getting well at home, and I had just gotten drafted by the Packers. It was time to adjust my mind to trying to make the team.

CHAPTER 8: Going to Camp

Nicole was gaining her strength back, starting to get up and walk again. She had been in the bed for the last couple of months. That May was my first minicamp, which was the first time the NFL team you were drafted by got a chance to bring you to the team facility and get a closer look at you. Being a country boy from Tallahassee, FL, it was amazing to be in a NFL facility, when there were thousands of players looking for this same opportunity. I went to minicamp thinking there was nothing that anyone could teach me about football, and how wrong I turned out to be. People really don't have any idea about the business of making a NFL team. It is basically a human meat market, players coming and going every day. The learning curve of making a NFL team is steep. In order to make the team, you really have to focus on the small details of your game, such as technique and quickness. There is not much difference in the talent level of a first round pick and a seventh round pick, except that the seventh rounder has to perform right away, while the first rounder has more time to adjust because they have invested major money in him.

I return to Bowling Green, KY a better football player after just a week of training with the pros. I am thinking this is my chance to finally get out of poverty and give something back to my grandparents for loving a lost and confused little boy who they loved anyway. I started training every day: running, lifting weights, and working on pass coverage skills. All I wanted to do was make this team and be able to say thanks to my grandparents and my girl Nicole. It was so hurtful how many people in my family were secretly hoping that I wouldn't make it, but it goes with the fact that my mom was considered to be nothing, so why would they want to see her kids become something? I thank all of the people in my family who wished badly for me, because they gave me the motivation to drive my kids to be all they can be in life. The months keep passing. Real training camp is approaching soon, August to be exact. Being from a smaller school, the chips are stacked against me, but that didn't matter. I have the heart of a lion and the courage of a soldier. Bring it on! They don't know I will knock an opposing player's head off! Football is all I had growing up that made people respect me, even if it was only on the field.

I report to training camp with a chip on my shoulder. This is all for my grandparents and my girl Nicole, but it became clear, from day one almost, who they would keep on the team. Most people would have thrown in the towel, but not me. They will know I was here even if they release me, and I did just that, hitting any and everything that moved! I made it down to the last 9 players out of 96! I found myself on the plane headed back home with tears in my eyes, with the feeling of disappointment. I failed the two people who loved me most in life. Where do I go from here? I don't know, but I am going to dry these tears up and keep plugging. I never had that silver spoon in my mouth anyway. My granny had a saying, "It's your little red wagon, you can pull it or push it," meaning: are you going to get back up or just lay there and feel sorry for yourself? I am pulling it! I am back at square one, planning my next move, and that is hopefully to get signed by this new football league that was starting up in the spring, The World Football League.

My agent starts working on getting me signed to the league. It was hard, but the contract finally arrived for me to sign. I'm back on top with a new opportunity to continue my dream of playing football. Even though no upfront money was involved, I was thankful for another chance to play football. There's only one problem: my hopes were so high on making the Packers team, that when they released me, it took some of the wind out of my sail, leaving me feeling burned out and drained. A few months would pass, and I was drafted by the Montreal Machine of the World Football League. It turned out to be a bad situation. I was on a team where my position coach had a couple players that played for him in college at Pittsburgh, playing the same position as me, and he never gave me a shot to make the team. So I am headed back home once again, but it didn't hurt like being released by Green Bay.

    I return to Tallahassee, and I am back in Bowling Green, KY after about a year. I was thankful for the time spent at Green Bay, but most of those guys couldn't play with the guys I played with at Western Kentucky. There was a lot of soft, hold my hand type players and coaches there. That's why most of them didn't have long careers. Playing at Western, I met guys who formed a bond for life with each other. Not everybody was the best of friends, but we enjoyed being around each other. In 1988, I would have put our team up against any division 1 team in the nation, if we would have had the same number of scholarships. We had many division 1 players. These guys changed my life in the fact that a whole team could be as one, and I tell you from personal experience, we knew how to rock the house during a football game.

CHAPTER 9: Daddy's Big Girl

I am back in Bowling Green, KY just hanging out. I still have some money, and I'm staying up late every night and sleeping late every morning. Then low and behold, my girlfriend was pregnant with the greatest thing to happen to me: Porsha Alexandria Martin. I realized the need to start working, so I was able to land a job with the United States Postal Service, but I still wasn't mature enough to work that job. I was required to work six days a week, and once a month, seven days, and it's all at night, so I quit. We are still alright because my girl was working, but I got another factory job at G.E. Electric Co. I worked there for a few months, and then things changed. My baby girl was born. And guess what, I'm going all in for the pretty little girl that kept daddy strong when he felt like he wanted to give up. I remember how I was treated growing up, so I have to stay around and protect her with everything I have. This was my baby, man! It's amazing how happy we were just to have each other.

Our first apartment was a house that someone had divided into a duplex. The apartment floors went up and down like a roller coaster, but I was so thankful to have them. My wife and I had broken up for about a year on account of my foolishness. I got her back and a brand new baby girl, who I called T.T., and I am in love with my baby. I come up with a plan for her life with the help of God. I found her a good daycare where she can start learning early in life. I am going to teach her everything about life, good and bad. I will be the example. Everywhere I went, my baby girl went with me. Daddy was so proud of her already, and she was still a baby. Having my daughter slowly opened my eyes to the fact that, no matter what, I couldn't go missing out of her life. I would rather be dead and buried than to be without my T.T. Writing this brings tears to my eyes thinking about her.

My baby was growing at a rapid rate. I could see that she was going to be big, tall, and pretty. We were still living in Bowling Green, KY., and my wife's mother passed before T.T. was born, so I am feeling even more protective of my wife and daughter. I hate that my daughter didn't get to meet one of the greatest women in the world, her maternal grandmother. My wife and I move back into the house with her dad, who is struggling with his wife dying. He then was diagnosed with cancer, and later had a stroke and was put into a nursing home. He only lived a day in the nursing home after being placed there. Now, things were really complicated. After his funeral, her family decided to sell their childhood home. What a mistake! It's funny how God knows everything. I was ready to leave

Bowling Green. There was no future there, but I knew she wouldn't leave if her parents hadn't died and her family hadn't decided to sell their home. I couldn't leave without them, and she was so broken hearted over the selling of the house. She moved to Tallahassee with me where I grew up. At this point in my life, I wanted to start a career, and provide for my wife and daughter.

Hanging out had lost some of its thrill. It was time to get committed. Shortly after her dad passed, we had a small, but really nice wedding. We moved back to Tallahassee, and I am feeling very protective of them. At home, they kept a lot of drama going, and my wife and daughter weren't getting caught up in that mess. Arriving back home, we relaxed for a week, and then we started looking for jobs. I was a little concerned about my wife's mental state, having to leave her home town so soon after her parents passed away. My daughter started kindergarten two years after we moved there, and she was smart as a whip. It felt so good for her to be so smart, because people have always looked at me as being dumb. I started early teaching her how to be a lady and earn respect for herself. My old high school coach was able to help me land a job at my high school. I worked 7 to 5 Monday through Friday, and went to the Fire Academy from 6:30 till 10, and all day on Saturday. I am committed to providing a better life for my daughter, and for her to be able to tell people where her dad works and be proud about it. I finished the Fire Academy and finally got hired with the local fire department. What an eye opening experience! It was very racially divided: forty blacks compared to about 300 whites. Most of the white guys wouldn't even speak to me, and I went to school with some of them. But so what, this wasn't about me. It's about my daughter. Remember, I said God knows everything.

Before I got hired in Tallahassee, I had done all my testing for the Atlanta Fire Department, and just when I started hating to go to work, Atlanta called and offered me a job! It was hard riding a fire truck and living with three guys who hated the site of me. I would bring food to work, and they would throw it away and pretend they didn't know who did it. I had to stand the rain for my wife and daughter. Later on, you will find out why God moved me from the Tallahassee Fire Department.

After about two years, we moved to Atlanta. I am not showing it, but I am really afraid, not knowing what to expect with only one cousin in Atlanta. I had to send my wife and daughter ahead of me to Atlanta because Atlanta kept pushing my start date back, again, and again, and again. Now I am really sad not seeing them every day. I rode the bus to go and see them. My car wasn't road worthy. Please don't think I am perfect at this point, but I am putting up a hell of a fight, trying to figure it out on the fly, on how to be a good husband and daddy. Daddy's little girl is in the 1st grade and blowing school, and any standardized test, out of the water! They can't pass judgment on my baby girl. There was one instance where my daughter was sick, and I wasn't in Atlanta. It brought tears to my eyes. I am used to being there for my baby.

I finally started my job with the Atlanta Fire Department. It was challenging going into the fire academy for the second time in about 3 years, but I was growing as a man, in the big city, and I have to handle my business and protect my wife and daughter. There was a lesson to be learned on my move from one fire department to the next, and that was everything that glitters isn't gold. Coming to the ATL, thinking everything was state of the art and up to date, that wasn't the case. But Atlanta allowed me to advance up the ranks, and my old department only allowed certain people of color to advance. In the beginning, in Atlanta, it felt like it was us against the world. No matter what happens, my daughter is the number one priority. She was very responsible and caring as a little girl. I knew all my energy and efforts would be invested in positioning her to be successful in life. She was growing and getting smarter by the day. We will visit her later in the book.

CHAPTER 10: Power Move

It is around September 1999, and my training at the fire academy is near the end. I have plans of starting my own janitorial service once they place me in a station, and boy, did they place me in the busiest station in Atlanta! But I am a man, and steadily growing. I can handle it. I start working a firefighter's schedule of 24 hours on, with 48 hours off. I didn't have any money. My wife had about 50 dollars on her credit card. I used that to buy my very first business license for the janitorial service. My motivation was so strong for my business. I didn't have a truck, so I hauled the equipment around in the trunk of my 1981 '98 Oldsmobile. People are always talking about starting their own businesses, but I promise you, you never worked that hard before in your life. All of the rewards and problems are yours. Still, at this point, I am motivated to make my business work. While working in Tallahassee at the fire department, every 3 months we came in at 7:00pm, and later that night, we were required to strip and wax the floors of the station. A friend of mine was really good at stripping and waxing floors, so I paid attention, asked questions, and learned how to strip and wax. I didn't have any money to buy equipment, so I started renting from Home Depot and anywhere that had what I needed for the job. One thing about me, I have never met a stranger. If you know or have something that interests me, I will ask you about it, and that's what I started doing. Everywhere I went, the first thing I did was look down at the floors. When me and my family were out together, if your floors were in bad shape, I would find out who I needed to talk to about them. Some people would decline the offer to talk, some would say come back another day, and you could bet, I would be back on that day and on time. The first job I picked up was at a locally owned Goodyear Tire Auto Shop. I did a good job but lost my shirt on the deal. I didn't make any money, but my motivation was high, and that one job was the encouragement that the dream could be achieved.

After a month or two, I am maintaining the Goodyear and picking up other accounts. Now I have gotten into the total janitorial business. We bought a computer, and a business program that allowed me to print invoices and estimates. I am growing in my business and as a man. My wife and daughter will have a great life. If there is any man out there who has been told that they are dumb and can't do something, get up and do something about it. Now my business is growing, but I'm still not growing or maturing in the family aspect of my life. I'm making plenty of money, but still hanging out and making bad decisions. If I am not at the fire station and somebody needs a floor done, I am the one to service it for them.

Growing up, I never dreamed of owning my own home. When we moved to Atlanta and I saw people who looked like me who owned fine homes and drove nice cars, that was encouragement for me and the evidence that we made the right decision. This day would forever change my life. I went into a real estate office and was waiting to speak with the owner about stripping & waxing his floors. While waiting, he was on the phone, and he says, "Even though you had a bankruptcy, we were still able to get you approved for a home loan." At that time, a bomb went off in my head! I said, "My God, if she can get approved, surely I can." When he got off of the phone, I asked him about stripping and waxing his floor, he agreed, and my next question was, "What do I need to do to get qualified for a home loan?" He told me to bring him certain documents, and he would pull my credit, and we would talk. I didn't know anything really about credit, but I left his office dancing. Just to have a chance at getting a home was so exciting to me. I really didn't know what to expect. A country boy like me never had anyone explain credit to me, but I knew my wife and daughter would be proud of me if this could be done. That was all that mattered to me.

A few months would pass, and then the phone call came from my real estate agent saying, "You got approved." Tears came to my eyes. We took a chance and moved away from family, and now my wife and daughter will have their own home. It's not necessary for me. I am a simple person. It doesn't take much to make me happy. Isn't this is what a husband and father is supposed to do, provide for his family? I try to teach my wife and kids this simple fact: never assume anything, go and ask questions, and find out the facts. If I had assumed I couldn't get approved for a home loan, we wouldn't be moving. Thank you Lord for blessing us! Now let's talk about having favor with God.

I need a truck for my business. It's growing too fast to carry all my equipment in the trunk of my car, plus my car won't pass the Georgia emissions test. I can't have anyone pull my credit while things are being finalized for closing on our house. Lord, what am I going to do? Driving down the street, I see a vehicle repossession lot that has a 1995 Ford F150 on it. I stopped and asked was it for sale and the guy said that it was. I explained my situation with the house and my credit, and put $500 down to hold it, not knowing if someone would finance a truck along with a house. I did it anyway. Everything is moving along; our home closing is coming up soon. I'm still acquiring

Scars — Chapter 10

more and more business accounts: doctor's offices, convenient stores, funeral homes, etc. I am making plenty of money just a one man show. My wife still isn't really excited. She doesn't really believe that we will be buying our own home. She took her time helping me with the documents we needed to get approved. We both came from places where dreams aren't very high. I will keep on keeping on. My love for her and my daughter runs deep.

The closing date is finalized. We go to closing, and there is a small problem. I had agreed to let the wife of the guy that did my loan be our agent, but the lady who showed us the house we bought stayed in my wife's ear about letting her be our agent, and she was the agent for the people selling the house also. Is she crazy? My wife tries to convince me to let her be both of our agents. That didn't work. We get to the closing table, and our agent starts arguing about the percentages they should get off the sale. I got pissed off and told them all, right in front of the lawyers that this should be one of the happiest days of my wife's life, and they were arguing about percentages. I am taking this family business very seriously. Remember, I am afraid of failing. Many people believe that we have made a mistake moving to Atlanta. We complete the closing, and we receive the keys and a garage door opener. I can't believe we are moving on up like George and Weezy on the Jeffersons.

I'm feeling great about myself, but there's still a problem. I need that truck that is on hold. The next day I go to the credit union and apply for a $10,000 car loan. Two days later, I am approved! Thank You Jesus for watching over us! That same day, the U-Haul moving truck pulls up in the yard. We start loading our belongings, just me and a friend from the fire academy. We finally got everything moved into the new home. Later that night, I asked my wife what took her so long to get the documents together we needed, and she said, "I didn't think we would get approved." I said, "I didn't either." But for her and my daughter, I was willing to try and put it all in God's hands. It is hard to describe the sense of accomplishment I felt that first night at our new house; the expressions on my wife and daughter's faces were priceless. The next day our daughter started her new school. We finally got everything unpacked. Things were moving along pretty well, and out of nowhere, my wife's transmission goes out on her car. Lord, what am I going to do now? We just got a new house and a new truck. No one is going to approve me for another car loan. Remember what happens when you have favor with God, and it is your due season. I prayed about it and went to the credit union for the second time in about 4 months. Three days later, I check on the decision, and thank you Lord, it was approved! Sometimes, a man is afraid just like anyone else, but a sign of a true man is that a boy does what he wants, and a man does what he has to do for the greater good of his family. A man doesn't stand on something to prove a point that may injure his family; he will give up being right to be happy.

Now we are living in west Atlanta. My business is growing even faster. I pick up 10 convenient stores, all the way up in North Georgia, Dalton, and Cartersville, about 50 miles north of Atlanta. During this time, my daughter is really growing tall, so I asked her if she ever thought about playing basketball. She said, "No because I can't be pretty." So I saw this magazine with Lisa Leslie in it modeling and playing basketball. I showed it to her, and said, "Look, you can play basketball and still be pretty." A basketball player was born! I immediately signed her up for recreation basketball, and she really didn't like to play, but she met some friends and they gave out snacks after the game, which made her want to go to the games, so that was fine with me. My plan worked! She played recreation basketball for a few years, and then she started playing AAU basketball at 9 years old.

At this time, I was working my fire department job and running my business, but my mom and brothers are having it pretty hard back at home for some reason. I felt the need to help them out, because people always labeled us as not turning out to be anything good in life, and I remember how we were treated as children growing up. I love my brothers, and only want the best for them and my mom. I started thinking about the fact that neither one of my brothers had anything going on but me. So I was wondering if my mom died, who would have to bury her? The answer is me. I contacted a life insurance company and had them go to my mom's house to do a physical exam. It was a relief to know my mom would have life insurance. A couple of weeks passed, and I make contact with the insurance company to find out if we could complete the paperwork. They told me that my mom was denied insurance. I called my mom and asked her what the problem was, and she said it was something with her blood, but she wouldn't tell me what. I eventually forgot about it and continued on with my life.

Every night I was off from the fire department, I loaded my truck up, and went out and do my janitorial jobs. This particular night, my grandmother called and said that my brother is in the jail infirmary, and he had been there for a couple of days with massive injuries, where two guys threw him off a second story balcony at a hotel head first. They really didn't know what condition he was in at the time, but he had a bond. I asked my grandmother to bond him out, if she had the money, and I would pay her back as soon as I got there. Quickly grabbing some clothes, I take off to Tallahassee. When I walked in my mom's house, he was laying on the couch, bandaged from head to toe. For days, they gave him no pain medicine, because he had drugs in his system. My brother suffered; tears came to my eyes. I stayed in Tallahassee until Sunday, caring for my brother. I bought his medicine, and changed his bandages. That Sunday, I told him once he got able to ride, he was coming home with me. After a few weeks, I went and picked him and my cousin up. I also had another cousin who came for the summer to stay with us. He was in college and wanted to earn some money working with me. Before my brother could leave home, I had to ask his probation officer to give him permission; he agreed with me that he needed change before he got himself killed. There were some conditions he had to meet; he had to take a drug test once a week and fax the results to her office, no alcohol, and no police contact. The drug test was $50.00 a week that I had to pay.

On the way back to Atlanta, I looked down at my brother's feet, and the shoes he had on were in bad shape. When we got in town, I took him shopping for clothes and shoes. I wanted him to feel good about himself and to know that I really loved him. He really had to keep himself straight. When he got thrown over the balcony, the doctors found crack in his pocket.

Now I have three employees. So I began picking up even more accounts. There had always been a demand for my services, but not having the people made it impossible. Now I could handle the work. Everything was going great! He sometimes made me nervous, because he was known to loan vehicles and run off for days at a time. He never did that to me. We were making all kinds of money! He was very good at supervising other people. He was making $600 a week, and life was great! My wife and daughter were spoiled to death. I told my brother if he could not be trusted with everything I had then I really didn't need him, because it was hard enough being in Atlanta with no family. I knew he had a court date coming up, and he would have to go back home.

My daughter was in Tallahassee at the time. I told him he could drive my truck and pick up my daughter and bring her back with him. I must admit, the situation made me nervous, but I wanted to trust him like no one else had. I came home from the fire station that morning. I had been fighting fire all night. I

Scars — Chapter 10

talked with him, and he and my cousin got in the truck and left. Later that night, I called my grandmother to see if anybody had seen him; this is around 6:00pm. He left Atlanta at 9:00am that morning. Now I am really nervous! Finally he showed up, and grandma said he had alcohol on his breath, but I stayed cool, giving him the benefit of the doubt. At about 10:00pm, I get a call from my cousin who rode to Tallahassee with my brother; he is now in jail! He's mad because he had an old warrant for his arrest in Tampa, FL, and my brother had driven to an area of town known for heavy drugs, and the police stopped them, ran their names, and they arrested him. He then tells me why it took so long for them to get to Tallahassee. My brother was visiting areas known for drugs all the way from South Georgia to Tallahassee. He knew many people in South Georgia. That pissed me off! My stomach started boiling! Now I was worried about my truck. My mom and aunt went to look for him with no success. Later that night, my aunt decided to go over to the hotel where he was thrown off the balcony. There he was with some girl sitting in my truck. She told him that I wanted my truck brought back to my grandmother's house and parked. He took off trying to lose her. Finally giving up, he got out of my truck and left it running in the middle of the street. She had to go and get my mom to drive it to my grandmother's house. I was hurt to my soul, believing and trusting in him when no one else would. My younger cousin went back to college, and everyone else was gone now. There was no one staying with me helping me with my business. I had to continue on with my business by myself. I never saw my brother alive again.

During all the drama, my baby brother is doing a life sentence in prison. He has been there for two or three years at this point. I never really understood why I felt the need to try and help everyone. I just wanted to see my brothers make it in life. You can want the world for a person, but if they don't want it, it's no good. My big brother soon made his third trip to prison. Now I had two brothers and both of my sons in prison. The idea of this situation had me feeling like there was a curse on my family. Some days I would be so depressed thinking about how many family members I had in prison. Finally, my mom went to the doctor, and a bomb exploded in my life! She is very sick ! I could not stop crying. You mean to tell me, my mom is going to die? Lost and upset, I was very confused. It seemed like we were being punished for some reason. I have to figure this thing out. She told me her medicine was $900 a month, and she had no insurance. Somehow, I have to get my mom's medicine. This is not her death sentence! It seems like everything falls on me. I am not even the oldest child! Some may wonder, after all the things my mother put me through, why would I be so concerned with what happened to her. It's simple: she's my mom, and I still love her dearly. I started sending her the $900 dollars and other money to pay some of her bills. After a few months, it became so stressful. I still had my family. Sometimes I would break down and cry. At the same time, my brothers who were in prison needed money, and my sons needed money. The lord always had his hands on me. This could have easily driven me over the edge. I felt bad because all of this energy was being put towards my mom, who at one time in my life had abandoned me, when my grandmother who raised me wasn't getting any attention. My grandmother has nine kids. Seven of the nine are pretty successful. My mom only has me, so what do I do? Well it comes a time, no matter how things may turn out, when a person has to live with themselves and do what they think is right. Even though she abandoned me and didn't treat me like her son at times, I wasn't going to treat her the same way.

CHAPTER 11: All or Nothing

Everywhere my daughter went to play, we were there. My wife would be there most of the time, but she worked retail, and her schedule was crazy sometimes. My job was going well; I got promoted to Sergeant, moving up the ladder. My two brothers were doing time, so trying to provide for my mom and give my brothers money is really getting stressful. A couple years passed, and one of my brothers gets out of prison. He hits the streets again; this was his third time in prison. I was hoping he would slow down and get a job. He was only interested in hitting the streets and doing crack. My best friend was getting married in Charlotte, NC. We went to Tallahassee and dropped off the kids, went to Charlotte, came back, and stayed a week. My brother never tried to see me once. That really hurt me.

April 19, 2006, I was sitting in my room at the fire station studying for the upcoming Lieutenants test, when something told me to call him. I called my mom's house, and she had just left. Her boyfriend told me an old girlfriend of my brother's had called her, and said that my brother had gotten shot. The last thing he said to me was that they had covered him up with a white sheet to keep him warm. Working where I work, that was a bad sign. Immediately, I called next door to my grandmother's house and asked if she knew anything about my brother getting shot. She said to call her back in a few minutes. She called my aunt. When I called back, they were rushing out headed to where he was. I immediately fell on my knees beside my bed and started praying. After praying for a while, I got up and sat on the side of the bed and waited to hear something. My stomach was boiling, and I was nervous. I sat there for about 45 minutes, and then the phone rang with a strange number. I was scared to answer it. I just looked at the phone, finally answering it. The first thing I heard was my momma and grandma crying, and then someone said, "He's gone." The tears rushed to my eyes like a machine was making tears for my eyes. My brother had only been out of prison 3 weeks. The feeling was like a cold numb feeling. I didn't know what to feel. My knees were weak. My brother, who I love with all my heart, was dead. Why he was killed was never really discovered. There was an arrest of a twenty-one year old street thug who witnesses said did it, but he walked away from it, because no one who was a witness was credible enough to put on the stand. They all were drug addicts or had a rap sheet. My brother was sitting in his car when a guy came up to the passenger side and shot in the window. He quickly jumped out of the car and ran up on the porch of the crack house he hung out at most of the time. One of his so called friends slammed the door in his face. There's no honor in a den of thieves. He then ran back off of the porch and was running across the parking lot of a body shop. The guy shot him three more times, one in his lung, one in his spine, and another in his stomach. There was a sheriff on his way home who saw my brother running, then walking, then stumbling. The sheriff pulled over. He fell right beside the driver side front tire and died before the officer could get out of his car.

I went over to my Captain's bedroom with tears in my eyes, and told him I had to go, that my brother had been murdered. On my way home, I couldn't stop crying, thinking about when he was living with me and all the times I talked to him, trying to help him. I didn't know it would happen this way, but I knew something was going to happen. The pitcher goes to the well a long time, but it finally gets broken. You get away with things a long time, but it eventually catches up with you. On the way home from the station, my brother's best friend called me very upset, crying so hard, I could barely understand him. He asked what we were going to do about it. At that point, I couldn't even feel anything. It seemed like a bad dream. My mom had to wait on scene to sign for them to move his body. She was very upset when we spoke on the phone. All my thoughts shifted to my older brother who was in the county jail. I didn't want him to see it on the news, so I told my grandmother to tell our cousin, who was like a brother to me, to go to the jail and tell my brother. My cousin worked for the Sheriff's department. That night I got no sleep, pondering many things such as, if we were going to pay for the Department of Corrections to bring my little brother.

The next day, I drove to Tallahassee. I felt all alone. One brother was dead, and my other two were locked up. Growing up, they were all that I knew, but I had to be strong for my mom and grandmother. Grandma was taking it really hard. She took us in as small children and worked to raise us. Thinking to myself, I wished at least one of my brothers was there to take the walk through this tragedy with me. Everyone I saw around town had their own version of what happened that night. Who cares, it's not going to bring him back! The day my brother died, my mom was getting on to him about going in the streets so much. She said he looked her in the eyes and said, "Momma, I am tired!" Making his funeral arrangements was really hard. We picked out a gold casket, his favorite color. It hurt so badly that someone gunned my brother down. This is where I know growth had happened in my life. Years ago, I would have wanted to avenge my brother's death. It's not worth it all. I am not saying there weren't struggles with those thoughts to do something crazy! The funeral plans were complete. I drove to Atlanta and back to Tallahassee all in one day, which is an 8 hour trip. It is now Thursday, and Saturday is the funeral. It still feels like a bad dream. I woke up early Saturday morning thinking about how my mom and grandmother would handle the funeral. A couple years earlier, my brother said to me that when I left and went to college, he became lost, because I wasn't around to be with him. When he said that to me, I didn't know what to say or do. This is my older brother, and I never knew he looked at me in that way.

As the time drew nearer to attend the funeral, my heart started beating faster. There was nothing more I could have done to help my brother. Sitting out front on the patio, the first family car from the funeral home pulled up: a black limousine that seats about ten adults. Now everything was starting to seem real. On April 28, 2006, family was arriving to line up for that horrifying ride to the church about 3 miles away. In the family car, the mood was as if we all were spaced out; our minds were gone away from our bodies. The procession started moving toward the church. As we stopped to turn in, there was a navy blue hearse parked on the corner, and I started to cry, knowing that hearse was carrying my brothers body. We lined up outside of the church to walk in and view his body and start the funeral; all I could think about is how much he would be missed. Walking in seeing his body lying there, I felt a little light headed but managed to get things back together for the service. I am the saddest man in the world. Everyone finally gets seated, and the funeral began. Thinking to myself, I will never see him again, staring at his casket, going through different emotions, I was so angry, sad, and depressed. My brother's best friend was supposed to speak, but was too upset to do it. They wanted to skip that part of the service, and before I knew it, I had stood up and said, "No, I will do it!" I just felt the need to say some words about my brother. The best part was that I got a chance to tell him that I loved him with a packed church watching, not really remembering the other things I said. The time came to push him out to the hearse. When he came by my seat, I wanted to tell them to STOP and just let me sit with him for a while. We loaded up in the family car. The procession started on our way to the grave site. I remember looking out of the rear glass, and there were cars as far as the eye could see. I thought to myself, "Man, I didn't know the four Martin brothers were that popular." Arriving at the grave site, and seeing the grave dug reinforced the fact that my brother won't be coming home anymore. I miss my brother so much. I feel very sad and blue. No mother should have to bury her child. I knew my mom was thinking about those years she missed with her boys, and now she's burying one of them. My dad didn't even make an effort to come to his funeral. His exact words were, "let the dead bury the dead." That made me mad, but why should it? That's the way we were treated growing up.

Now it's time to go back to Atlanta. Now I am feeling rage that this guy killed my brother. Trying to control my emotions driving home was very hard, wondering if there was anything more I could have done to save my brother. In the months following his death, I started going off the deep end. Life didn't mean the same to me anymore. I was hanging out, drinking more, and hanging around people who I shouldn't have been, searching for the answer in all the wrong places. The biggest problem was that we knew who killed him, and I wanted to drive home and put him in my trunk, but I had been slowly maturing over the years, and I had a wife and kids depending on me. But the pain didn't seem to go away. It felt like I was losing my mind. Remember earlier in the book when I talked about it being a blessing to leave the Tallahassee Fire

Department? The first engine that got to my brother after he was shot and killed was E1, the same fire truck that I rode while working in Tallahassee. It is very likely that I could have been on that engine when it pulled up to the crime scene. I would have lost my mind, who knows, maybe forever!

CHAPTER 12: It's Storming

Just as the title of this chapter suggests, after all of the heartbreak and pain, it had to get worse! I basically talked to my mom every day, and suddenly, she stopped coming to the phone when I called. My niece, god brother, and oldest brother would always tell me she was sleep every time I called. This went on for about three or four weeks. My grandmother told me that my mom was really sick, and I needed to come home. They were putting the best on the outside, thinking they were hiding or protecting her, but she was actually dying. Tired of being told different stories, my family and I took off to Tallahassee. What was found upon our arrival made me want to get physical with them. My mom had lost 25 to 30 pounds. I talked with my aunt who lived in Texas at the time, and she went to Tallahassee and got my mom admitted to the hospital in ICU. You wonder why I didn't get her admitted to the hospital; she was still in her right mind and refused. Anytime a person is of sound mind, they can make their own decisions. I went back to Atlanta and came back to Tallahassee a week later. Walking in her room almost killed me! I had never seen so many IV drips in my life! My mom was on a ventilator. We had to put on HEPA masks, gloves, and gowns to protect her immune system. Everyone had written her off for dead, especially that sorry husband of hers. My family was arguing back and forth. I must admit, it didn't look good. Sunday, I decided to go home and wait for the phone call that she had passed. What a long four hour ride back to Atlanta that was! The next day, I called that afternoon to check on her, and in the back ground, I could hear her talking! I couldn't believe that she was conscious and talking, after looking like it was over for her. Eventually, she went home, but had to learn how to walk again, which I really credit God and my older brother with. He worked with her and nursed her back to health, when there was talk in the family to put her in a nursing home. Thumbs up to my oldest brother for believing in her when everyone had written her off, including me.

CHAPTER 13: The Struggle

After my brother's death, and dealing with my mom's situation, I was feeling like I cared too much about family situations. I found myself slipping away mentally. The pressure of trying to help so many people had gotten the best of me. The first medical call my station ran once I returned to work, was a shooting of a guy who, to me, looked a lot like my brother. If I didn't have a family to take care of, that probably would have been my last day working as a fire fighter. Every day was a struggle to stay mentally sane. I was hanging out drinking, trying to make myself not care about the pain I was feeling at the time. It had gotten really hard for me to report for duty, fearing the medical calls we may encounter during the shift. The hardest times trying to deal with my mom's situation and my brother's death, would always be in the morning riding to work and coming back home the next morning, sometimes crying myself all the way to work and back home.

This was a miserable time in my life; trying to deal with things on my own wasn't working. There were thoughts of suicide. The pain was that great! All the feelings and thoughts of the way I grew up made me feel as if nothing good would ever come of my life. Working at the fire department was the last place I wanted to be spending 24 hours of my time. Every shift was a struggle to complete. It is very hard to explain the feelings and emotions inside my mind and heart at that time. I wished for another chance to talk to my brother, and then it happened! I was sleeping one night, and my brother came to me. The first thing I said to him was, "What are you doing here?" He replied, "I only got shot." He had on this white shirt that snapped at the shoulder, and he reached up and unsnapped it and said, "Look." It looked like two nickel sized burn wounds. When I woke up, I was standing on my front porch in my boxers. Through all of this, the police had made an arrest, but it did little to comfort me. There were so many versions of what and why it happened. Dealing with the State Prosecutors office was a task; listening to the things that were being said about my brother, most of them were negative. I just didn't know how or what to feel!

My oldest daughter was in high school doing really well in school and basketball. I still had my two youngest children, trying to find a way to balance everything, fighting off the evil demons every day. Things between me and my wife were really really shaky, all because of the situations going on with my family and me. Looking back on those times, it was very unfair for innocent people to suffer for things they had nothing to do with. It was unfair for me to suffer, and this was my family. Still trying to maintain my sanity and wait for God to rescue me, I knew he would. I just didn't know the time or place he was coming. I was hanging around some bad people in some bad places. Many times we have to find a way to continue getting up and fighting another day. First, I must give all honor to the Lord Jesus Christ, he had mercy on me, not to let me lose my mind, or go and do something stupid. The responsibility of having a wife and children kept me trying to hold on to life, when it really didn't matter to me one way or the other whether I lived or died. It's like the old saying goes: *I was sick and tired of being sick and tired.* Every time I thought about letting my wife and kids down, it pushed me a little more to keep trying. There were many nights I sat outside my house and drank Hennessey, and I prayed and cried out to God to please help me. Many of you may question how could I be drinking and praying at the same time. Easy! The Lord says come as you are, and at that time, I was stripped of all pride and was as naked as I was when I came into this world. Even though things had gotten really bad, the Lord had to deal with me more harshly to whip me into better shape!

CHAPTER 14: Taking Things for Granted

The Lord was not pleased with me, he had to split my head to the white meat; he delivered what I call a shape up or ship out blow. In February 2008, he allowed me to be arrested on drug charges that would forever change my life. I had caused problems within my home, due to all the problems going on around me. Never making any excuses, I should have realized not to put that type of pressure on myself. I never thought that I was just one person trying to solve everybody's problems creating more for myself in the process. Remember when I said that being at the fire station wasn't where I wanted to be? God fixed it where I didn't have to go for a year and two months. I got picked up by some narcotics agents who had caught a person I knew with drugs, and yes, I hung around this person and others, who were doing things they shouldn't have been. It was my entire fault! I should have known better than to be in those places. February 3, 2008, I went to jail with possession of narcotics charges. They didn't find anything in my car, or in my house, but found it in someone else's house, who I had let get cable in my name. I am not here to justify those charges, because I never even went to court on those charges; they were dropped.

There is a bigger picture to focus on, and that is something that seemed so bad at the time but turned out to be a big blessing. Sometimes, we have this sense of entitlement, that we are untouchable. I wasn't feeling that way. The situations had me thinking with an unclear mind. I went to jail on the 3rd, and the police thought they were embarrassing me, because they arrested me in front of my oldest daughter at my son's daycare, but he didn't see me get arrested. What they allowed my daughter to see was a man who was standing strong in a bad situation, her dad. The first thing they did was called my job and painted this picture of me selling drugs, which my job bought. They told my wife I was living a double life, trying to divide us and turn us against each other, thinking she knew something to tell them about me. Don't they know, if I was doing something, I would never jeopardize my family? I don't think she realized what she said to them gave me the strength to fight through another bad situation. She told them, "No matter what y'all say, I am with him." My thinking at that point was let's go to jail, so I can start the process of getting out of this mess. After all their games and thinking they were scaring me, I was finally transported to the county jail, with the cops saying that I was going to jail without a bond. Was that supposed to make me act out or something? The next day I went to court for my bond hearing. My bond was $19,000 which 15% had to be paid for me to be released. All my thoughts were on my wife and kids and finding a job once I was out of jail. There was a guy in the holding cell with me who told me to call this certain bonding agency. I called and talked with them. They came over without any money in hand and bonded me out on my word of coming back the next day to pay them their money. Once released, I had $4 in my pocket. I hadn't had anything to eat in more than 24 hours. I went into the Bar B Q joint in front of the jail, got a pulled pork sandwich and a sweet tea, found a bad dog stick, and walked 12 miles home in the freezing cold of February with short sleeves and no jacket. The office of Professional Standards from the Fire Department came to the jail to inform me that on February 17, 2008, I would receive my last pay check. It was amazing how quick they did my suspension paperwork. But I had no time to cry over spilled milk. I walked all the way home pondering my next move. I have to find a job and continue taking care of my family. I didn't have the answers right then, but I was willing to go and find them.

It only took about two weeks to find another job, thanks to my cousin. The job I found was extremely hard and fast paced. I started off working on a conveyer belt line, loading shipping containers, and then at the end of the night I loaded eighteen wheelers with freight to be delivered. It was 10 to 14 hours a day, 6 days a week at $8.00 an hour, but I was thankful to have some sort of income coming into the house, knowing my case would take at least a year. So I tried to focus on the task at hand. A few months passed, and then I broke my ankle; that took my pay down to $260 a week of worker's compensation pay. Prayer and believing in God took care of us. That was all that I had on my side. I wasn't worried about my case, but very concerned. There had been many instances where the evidence was insufficient, but the person was still convicted. My biggest prayer to God was for him not to let my situation interrupt what my daughter was doing in school and basketball; she is my pride and joy. During all of the madness, the Fire Department sent me a certified letter stating that the Fire Chief had decided to terminate my employment, which I didn't respond to. Why put the horse before the cart? If they mailed me the letter, then his mind was made up, and I don't beg and plead for no reason. I don't want to seem as if I am bragging about the situation; this is just my way of showing people that you have to find a way to be strong when you feel like giving up.

There have been many times I felt like giving up, especially when everything I touched just crumbled into pieces, and you don't understand why this happens. Sometimes, it felt like I was about to smother to death with all the problems and

Scars — Chapter 14

thinking about how to get life right. Maybe there were times when my faith was shaken, but deep down in my heart, my faith in the Lord was very strong. Like that old church hymn says, *"Guess I'll run on, and see what the end will be."* Every day I woke up, there was the hope that this was the day the nightmare would be over, and that day came. The charges were dropped, and I went back to work at the Fire Department. I showed up out of nowhere with my paperwork from the courts, stating I was free and clear of this mess. This is a very important part of what people need to know in order to survive. Of course, when I reported back to work, the story had been told 1000 different ways, but you can't put any energy into all the talk. I was placed at our training academy for about a month, and a guy I knew said to me, "Keep your head up," as if I had something to be ashamed of. People get arrested all the time, but it doesn't mean they are guilty. I said to him, "Just me being back at work speaks for itself." Some people have too much pride; my skin is as thick as an alligator's skin. Remember, I wasn't supposed to be anything in life anyway! After being suspended for no reason, the city still pulled a trick on me. When it was time to pay me for my lost wages, they were able to punish me twice by taking $11,000 of my back pay money. As messed up as that was, it couldn't kill my spirits. While I was waiting for my situation to be resolved, my prayer to God was to let me get back in time to take the next Lieutenants exam. Not only did he answer my prayer, but out of 180 people, I came out number 36 on the list! This was one of the most challenging periods in my life. There were people in my family who were having a good time with the fact that I was having it really hard and the cops were trying to take my career from me, but I kept praying and looking up even if there were many cloudy days. There were people who took personal shots at me, but I was cool with it, because there will be people who will benefit from me sharing my story.

CHAPTER 15: What's for Me Is Just for Me

After returning to work, about a year later, I got promoted to Lieutenant and assigned to the Fire Marshall's Office. Many people didn't think I was deserving of the position, but the Lord said otherwise. I still have my wife and kids through all the ups and downs, all the tears, and crying out to God to keep me traveling the right road and to keep his arms of safety around me and my family. Every day, I got up asking him to allow my kids to grow up and be outstanding people of character. They are better off at their ages than I was, because they have a dad and mom that gives their all for them each and every day. I often get to work early and work on this book. For some reason, things seem much clearer to me early in the morning. I sit and remember all the bad times and the good times, dreaming about where I want our lives to be someday. I think about my big girl in college, giving it all she has. It brings tears to my eyes, because I am so very proud of her, and no one can pass judgment on what she will be in life like they did me, and still do at times. If this is the road the Lord would have me travel to get my kids there, then let's ride! I am constantly thinking, hoping, and praying that the Lord gives me the wisdom and strength to continue to be strong and keep my head up on my way to a better life.

My drive has been strengthened through my two younger kids: Peyton and Jerome III. These children have come at a point when the way I looked at life was changing dramatically. I call them my best buddies. They are involved in fast pitch softball, basketball, football, and baseball. Getting them from place to place is a challenge, but I love them so much, it doesn't matter. Many times, my motivation comes from trying to make sure they have the best possible chance to succeed. It is 99% about them, and 1% about me. Peyton is like an old soul that has been here before. Now, she is my little helper, doing all the little things to help me. Even if I am feeling down, she picks me back up. I taught Peyton that it is her responsibility to look out for her younger brother when they are away from home. It is time for here to go to middle school, and because of her, I feel good about him going to school by himself. She has taught him well. He will be fine. Jerome III (Trey) is the second coming of me. We are two spitting images of each other. When he was born, Trey stayed sick a lot, which worried me. He had breathing problems and acid reflux. As he got older many of his problems began to disappear. I guess he out grew the health problems. In school, he does really well, but he is in speech, just like I was. The difference is that he has me around to encourage him and let him know that there is nothing wrong with getting the help you need. I wanted help with my school work in high school, but was scared to ask, because people always laughed and said what I couldn't do, so I never asked. What a huge mistake! I make sure that me and my son talk about being proud and ask for understanding of the things he doesn't understand. We have real life conversations about life, and he is only 8 years old. I tell him about the things that happened to me growing up, and his eyes grow really big, and he asks a lot of questions. He is very athletic, even though he isn't going to be big like I was. My son has a deep love for the Lord. He is always talking about how he loves God. Trey really has to work hard in school, but I will never let anyone make him feel unworthy, because I use myself as the example for him to follow in his life. I tell him about my struggles in school and how I came up short by being ashamed. The Lord knows what we need even before we ask him for things. My day starts with praying to God for his help and keeping me strong and mentally healthy.

CHAPTER 16: Just Want to Give Thanks

Who would have thought that after all that has happened in my life, I would have a seat at the head of the table. The Lord answered my prayers in allowing me to get back on my job and make Lieutenant, but he has blessed me in a better way. He promoted me to the rank of Captain who oversees the world's busiest airport inspections sections. This is living proof that tough times don't last forever, but tough people do. There were times when I felt as if everything in life was going wrong, but getting up and trying life again the next day and praying without stopping has saw me through the hard times. Thinking back on all the people who betted against me, it really doesn't matter now. God has been better to me than I have been to myself. I never in my wildest dreams would have imagined sitting in meetings with top level executives and making decisions that are key to the operation of major airlines. Every day that I report to work and sit in my office, it reminds me of how a poor kid with all kinds of problems can overcome some of the worst situations in life. There was no way I would be here if it wasn't for the tests over the years; there can't be a testimony without a test! I challenge any person who is looking for a way to get on their feet to just keep looking up to the hills for your help, put one foot in front of the other, and believe that God will deliver you from the situation. It has to be understood that the journey will not be easy and having patience will be the ultimate test, because we want instant solutions to our problems. There were many times I thought that God had forgotten about me, but it didn't stop me from praying and still believing. God says that if you have faith as small as a mustard seed he will bless you, and my faith has been that small before. There are many people who are just like me, searching to find the strength to hold on; that strength only comes from having some type of relationship with God. If you don't have one, it will be in your best interest to get to know him.

I am proud of myself for being able to put my life on display, when years ago this would have never happened. It makes me proud to know that this will help someone live a more productive life. If I don't get another promotion I have seen the power of the Lord, power to whip me back in to shape, and the power to have mercy when I needed it most! Often I sit and wonder how does a person make it through bad times? There is no magic potion or simple answer; all a person can do is keep getting up and trying life over and over again. In my life, I have learned that everything that glitters isn't gold, meaning that when a person seems to have it all together, there are things about them that they wish would go away. For instance, many people who are rich and set financially could have kids who have a birth defect or something their money cannot fix. I believe that there is a trade-off with the Lord; he gives some things and he takes some away. Some people may struggle with finances, but their kids are healthy. I am just trying to give some understanding of why things happen in our lives.

CHAPTER 17: Real Talk for Men

We have to stop standing on the prehistoric pride of years ago. A man can't grow until he realizes that it's alright to feel and be afraid at times. I wasted many years denying my feelings and refusing to admit that there was great pain built up inside of me. How can a man continue to grow and make strides that will allow him to release the hurt in his heart? First, he must find something or someone who motivates him internally. Most men are afraid to open up and try and handle things differently. We stay connected to things that we are familiar with, like not letting anyone into our space of emotions. I cheated myself for years thinking the outward appearance of being hard was the way to handle things. All that did was allow the hurt from my childhood to build up to a point where it almost became unmanageable. I was scared to let people know how I felt as a child; this injured my character, my self-esteem, and my potential to excel in school and sports. Over the years, having a family slowly allowed me to drop that armor that I thought was necessary to survive. Being able to get past all the hurt and pain people had caused me allowed me to become more of a comfort to be around, and a more loving person with my family. Until you can get yourself together, lean heavily on the people around you — your wife, your kids — to keep yourself in the middle of the road. It takes many years for men to fully mature and figure things out. We need something around that means the world to us. For every man who is trying to take care of his family, life is like a jig saw puzzle: every piece has its place on the board of life. Being in Atlanta with no family, my mind is constantly churning on the next situation that may arise: the kids after school situation, sending money to my oldest daughter, making sure my wife has what she needs, etc. The responsibility never ends when we are trying to provide. There is nothing wrong with getting tired or having the feeling of being burned out, but there is a problem with giving up or walking away from your family. If those things had not happened to me as a child, I might not be as committed as I am to my family. Sitting on Thanksgiving Day 2012, watching my kids laughing and enjoying each other while their momma cooks the meal, is my reward for every situation that has to be figured out, and every morning I pray to the Lord to keep us under his protective shield.

How does a man keep himself from going insane with the pressures of standing up and providing for his family? First, he has to understand that he can't do it by himself. Pray and lean on the Lord. There has to be a plan and thoughts and dreams of what the vision is for his family. Try to determine what situations in your life need attention right away. I sit around asking the Lord when my time will come to be financially free. I don't know if it will ever come, but I am believing and putting forth the effort by not being lazy and working any extra job that is available. There are so many men like me around the world, who have learned everything on the fly, learning through mistakes and heartbreak. We can't continue to make the same mistakes over and over again; as my grandma would say, "crapping in the road and putting it on the dog." Our bad decisions can't be blamed on anyone but ourselves. The prisons are full of people just like me, but the Lord kept smiling on me even when he should have turned his back. Trying to describe the daily feelings of wanting to succeed in life, I can't find the words to explain my deepest thoughts. Describing what we feel is something men must practice daily. We would rather say forget it, or just totally shut down, than to try to explain how we are feeling. I don't want to stand still financially or mentally. These are things that prevent men from growing. Our kids need to see us grow and mature right in front of their eyes. Maybe this book is not for the fully matured man, but it's for us who are still trying to get it right.

CHAPTER 18: Children

    I can remember growing up and things would happen in my life that made me say, "I can't wait until I'm grown." Now here I am. Kids, remain a child as long as you can. There's nothing like just being responsible for going to school, getting good grades, and obeying your parents. Once you get grown, there is no going back. Every problem you may have is all yours. If I could go back in time, I wouldn't have been involved in the things that caused me problems later in life. Being a child that parents can be proud of is a precious gift to parents. I tell my 20 year old daughter all the time that she has only a few years to be a child and many to be grown. Had I remained young at heart, my twins wouldn't have gotten cheated out of having their dad around to show them the right way to go in life. At some point, the cycle has to be broken. I decided once grown, that the next children of mine would be the ones in my family to distance themselves from the things I knew about. I am very loving to them, but they follow a fine line. I am not on this new program of raising children; I am on the old program. My grandmother always said, "You can discipline your children, or the prison system will do it for you." Everything I know about life will be told to my kids, good and bad. You can't love your kids and know the game and not give it to them. Parents, stop begging your kids to behave, make them behave, because life can get better, or it can get worse. This book is not for those that have it all together, this book is for those who feel like they are the only ones that have had it hard in life, but are still getting up every day putting forth the very best effort possible! Even though times have been challenging, the Lord has blessed me to be married for 18 years, have a 20 year old daughter on a college basketball scholarship with a 3.5 GPA majoring in Biology, a 10 year old daughter who is really bright in school and a great athlete, and a son who is so far ahead of me when I was his age, and little old me: a 15 year veteran of the Atlanta Fire Rescue Department, now a Captain over Airport Inspection at the Hartsfield-Jackson Atlanta International Airport. Who would have ever thought it? Praise the Lord!!

CHAPTER 19: Give Life A Chance!

Chapter 18 was supposed to be the last chapter to this book, until my cousin's son committed suicide. Riding home on a Wednesday afternoon after work, my cousin called, and I could tell he was very upset, and he said, "One of my son's committed suicide this morning." The first word from my mouth was, "Why?" If most men would tell the truth, the thought has passed through their minds about committing suicide. There is a difference in contemplating suicide and the thought passing through your mind. A lot of men who look like me have been through some very difficult times whether it was prison, growing up without one parent, or both, or being judged by the color of your skin. It took about a week for his funeral to be held. That gave me time to do some quality soul searching. I have been to the point, many times, where life had just beat me down. The day he killed himself, I went over to my cousin's house, and to see his mom in the state of mind of trying to figure out why he did this, or was there more she could've done to prevent him from doing it, it was heart breaking. No parent should have to bury their child; their children should bury them.

When someone kills themselves, everyone around them is traumatized. I spoke about finding the motivation to keep getting up and trying to make this day better than yesterday earlier in the book, but I am going to break it down to the bone. Let's go all the way in on this one! I arrived at the funeral home about 9:15am, walked into the chapel, and there he was lying in a wooden casket. My mind was wondering what was going through his mind prior to him committing suicide. I walked up to view his body. After viewing his body, I took a seat about four rows from his casket, observing the reaction of everyone who came in to view him; some are crying, shaking their heads, and it was hard for some to leave his casket. I will never forget when the mother of two of his sons came down to view his body. She just stood and cried, while holding the three year old, with the five year old standing beside her. The three year old started reaching for his dad, so she leaned him over, and he lay in his dad's chest. That touched the bottom of my soul! The mother and the two boys sat two rows in front of me and my wife. The five year old understood what was going on: his dad was dead. Many people don't think that black males have a caring and sensitive side, but we do. It's just that along the way of life, so many people suppress this side, and it all but disappears. As the mom sat and continued to weep, the five year old started rubbing her shoulder, and then rubbed the back of her head as if he was saying to his mom that they would be alright. It was amazing to me, seeing him reach out to his mom in that manner, at that age. Looking at those two little boys made it clearer than ever, that I have got to stay around for my kids for as long as God lets me. It has been a week since the funeral, and those memories are still on my mind. All a man has these days is his faith in God and the motivation he draws from his wife and kids, or any person, place, or thing that gives him the desire to see another day. Every day I am hoping and praying that this is the day that brings everything together for me, but until that day arrives, I say to anyone who reads this book, "The race is not won by the swift, but by the one who endures." It won't be easy, but there is someone who is counting on you to stay around!